THE CONSTITUTION

as altered
to
31 October
1986

---

together with

Proclamation Declaring Establishment of Commonwealth

Letters Patent Relating to the Office of Governor-General

Statute of Westminster Adoption Act 1942
Australia Act 1986

Index

Australian Government Publishing Service
Canberra 1986

Printed in Australia by R. D. RUBIE, Commonwealth Government Printer, Canberra

Contents

COMMONWEALTH OF AUSTRALIA
CONSTITUTION ACT

with alterations of the Constitution made by

CONSTITUTION ALTERATION (SENATE ELECTIONS) 1906
(No. 1 of 1907)

CONSTITUTION ALTERATION (STATE DEBTS) 1909
(No. 3 of 1910)

CONSTITUTION ALTERATION (STATE DEBTS) 1928
(No. 1 of 1929)

CONSTITUTION ALTERATION (SOCIAL SERVICES) 1946
(No. 81 of 1946)

CONSTITUTION ALTERATION (ABORIGINALS) 1967
(No. 55 of 1967)

CONSTITUTION ALTERATION (SENATE CASUAL VACANCIES) 1977
(No. 82 of 1977)

CONSTITUTION ALTERATION (RETIREMENT OF JUDGES) 1977
(No. 83 of 1977)

CONSTITUTION ALTERATION (REFERENDUMS) 1977
(No. 84 of 1977)

Note.—Words and phrases inserted by the Constitution Alterations specified above are shown in the text in bold type, while new sections and paragraphs may be identified from the marginal notes showing them as inserted, added or substituted.

Omitted words and phrases are ruled through in the text; repealed sections are shown in full in the Notes commencing on page 36.

THE CONSTITUTION

As Altered to 31 October 1986

(See Note 1 on page 36)

TABLE OF PROVISIONS

CHAPTER I

THE PARLIAMENT

PART I—GENERAL

PART II—THE SENATE

TABLE OF PROVISIONS—continued

CHAPTER VI

NEW STATES

CHAPTER VII

MISCELLANEOUS

CHAPTER VIII

ALTERATION OF THE CONSTITUTION

SCHEDULE

Oath and affirmation of allegiance

THE CONSTITUTION

(63 & 64 VICTORIA, CHAPTER 12)

An Act to constitute the Commonwealth of Australia.

[9th July 1900]

WHEREAS the people of New South Wales, Victoria, South Australia, Queensland, and Tasmania, humbly relying on the blessing of Almighty God, have agreed to unite in one indissoluble Federal Commonwealth under the Crown of the United Kingdom of Great Britain and Ireland, and under the Constitution hereby established:

And whereas it is expedient to provide for the admission into the Commonwealth of other Australasian Colonies and possessions of the Queen:

Be it therefore enacted by the Queen's most Excellent Majesty, by and with the advice and consent of the Lords Spiritual and Temporal, and Commons, in this present Parliament assembled, and by the authority of the same, as follows:—

1. This Act may be cited as the Commonwealth of Australia Constitution Act.[1] *Short title.*

2. The provisions of this Act referring to the Queen shall extend to Her Majesty's heirs and successors in the sovereignty of the United Kingdom. *Act to extend to the Queen's successors.*

3. It shall be lawful for the Queen, with the advice of the Privy Council, to declare by proclamation[2] that, on and after a day therein appointed, not being later than one year after the passing of this Act, the people of New South Wales, Victoria, South Australia, Queensland, and Tasmania, and also, if Her Majesty is satisfied that the people of Western Australia have agreed thereto, of Western Australia, shall be united in a Federal Commonwealth under the name of the Commonwealth of Australia. But the Queen may, at any time after the proclamation, appoint a Governor-General for the Commonwealth. *Proclamation of Commonwealth.*

4. The Commonwealth shall be established, and the Constitution of the Commonwealth shall take effect, on and after the day so appointed. But the Parliaments of the several colonies may at any time after the passing of this Act make any such laws, to come into *Commencement of Act.*

operation on the day so appointed, as they might have made if the Constitution had taken effect at the passing of this Act.

Operation of the constitution and laws.

5. This Act, and all laws made by the Parliament of the Commonwealth under the Constitution, shall be binding on the courts, judges, and people of every State and of every part of the Commonwealth, notwithstanding anything in the laws of any State; and the laws of the Commonwealth shall be in force on all British ships, the Queen's ships of war excepted, whose first port of clearance and whose port of destination are in the Commonwealth.[3]

Definitions.

6. "The Commonwealth" shall mean the Commonwealth of Australia as established under this Act.

"The States" shall mean such of the colonies of New South Wales, New Zealand, Queensland, Tasmania, Victoria, Western Australia, and South Australia, including the northern territory of South Australia, as for the time being are parts of the Commonwealth, and such colonies or territories as may be admitted into or established by the Commonwealth as States; and each of such parts of the Commonwealth shall be called "a State."

"Original States" shall mean such States as are parts of the Commonwealth at its establishment.

Repeal of Federal Council Act.
48 & 49 Vict. c. 60.

7. The Federal Council of Australasia Act, 1885, is hereby repealed, but so as not to affect any laws passed by the Federal Council of Australasia and in force at the establishment of the Commonwealth.

Any such law may be repealed[4] as to any State by the Parliament of the Commonwealth, or as to any colony not being a State by the Parliament thereof.

Application of Colonial Boundaries Act.
58 & 59 Vict. c. 34.

8. After the passing of this Act the Colonial Boundaries Act, 1895, shall not apply to any colony which becomes a State of the Commonwealth; but the Commonwealth shall be taken to be a self-governing colony for the purposes of that Act.

Constitution.

9. The Constitution of the Commonwealth shall be as follows:—

THE CONSTITUTION.[1]

This Constitution is divided as follows:—

CHAPTER I.

THE PARLIAMENT.

PART I.—GENERAL.

1. The legislative power of the Commonwealth shall be vested in a Federal Parliament, which shall consist of the Queen, a Senate, and a House of Representatives, and which is herein-after called "The Parliament," or "The Parliament of the Commonwealth." *Legislative power.*

2. A Governor-General appointed by the Queen shall be Her Majesty's representative in the Commonwealth, and shall have and may exercise in the Commonwealth during the Queen's pleasure, but subject to this Constitution, such powers and functions of the Queen as Her Majesty may be pleased to assign to him. *Governor-General.*

3. There shall be payable to the Queen out of the Consolidated Revenue fund of the Commonwealth, for the salary of the Governor-General, an annual sum which, until the Parliament otherwise provides, shall be ten thousand pounds. *Salary of Governor-General.*

The salary of a Governor-General shall not be altered during his continuance in office.

4. The provisions of this Constitution relating to the Governor-General extend and apply to the Governor-General for the time being, or such person as the Queen may appoint to administer the Government of the Commonwealth; but no such person shall be entitled to receive any salary from the Commonwealth in respect of any other office during his administration of the Government of the Commonwealth. *Provisions relating to Governor-General.*

5. The Governor-General may appoint such times for holding the sessions of the Parliament as he thinks fit, and may also from time to time, by Proclamation or otherwise, prorogue the Parliament, and may in like manner dissolve the House of Representatives. *Sessions of Parliament. Prorogation and dissolution.*

Summoning Parliament.   After any general election the Parliament shall be summoned to meet not later than thirty days after the day appointed for the return of the writs.

First session.   The Parliament shall be summoned to meet not later than six months after the establishment of the Commonwealth.

Yearly session of Parliament.   **6.** There shall be a session of the Parliament once at least in every year, so that twelve months shall not intervene between the last sitting of the Parliament in one session and its first sitting in the next session.

Part II. The Senate.

PART II.—THE SENATE.

The Senate.   **7.** The Senate shall be composed of senators for each State, directly chosen by the people of the State, voting, until the Parliament otherwise provides, as one electorate.

But until the Parliament of the Commonwealth otherwise provides, the Parliament of the State of Queensland, if that State be an Original State, may make laws dividing the State into divisions and determining the number of senators to be chosen for each division, and in the absence of such provision the State shall be one electorate.

Until the Parliament otherwise provides there shall be six senators for each Original State. The Parliament may make laws increasing or diminishing the number of senators for each State,[5] but so that equal representation of the several Original States shall be maintained and that no Original State shall have less than six senators.

The senators shall be chosen for a term of six years, and the names of the senators chosen for each State shall be certified by the Governor to the Governor-General.

Qualification of electors.   **8.** The qualification of electors of senators shall be in each State that which is prescribed by this Constitution, or by the Parliament, as the qualification for electors of members of the House of Representatives; but in the choosing of senators each elector shall vote only once.

Method of election of senators.   **9.** The Parliament of the Commonwealth may make laws prescribing the method of choosing senators, but so that the method shall be uniform for all the States. Subject to any such law, the Parliament of each State may make laws[6] prescribing the method of choosing the senators for that State.

Times and places.   The Parliament of a State may make laws[6] for determining the times and places of elections of senators for the State.

10. Until the Parliament otherwise provides, but subject to this Constitution, the laws in force in each State, for the time being, relating to elections for the more numerous House of the Parliament of the State shall, as nearly as practicable, apply to elections of senators for the State.

Application of State laws.

11. The Senate may proceed to the despatch of business, notwithstanding the failure of any State to provide for its representation in the Senate.

Failure to choose senators.

12. The Governor of any State may cause writs to be issued for elections of senators for the State. In case of the dissolution of the Senate the writs shall be issued within ten days from the proclamation of such dissolution.

Issue of writs.

13. As soon as may be after the Senate first meets, and after each first meeting of the Senate following a dissolution thereof, the Senate shall divide the senators chosen for each State into two classes, as nearly equal in number as practicable; and the places of the senators of the first class shall become vacant at the expiration of ~~the third year~~ **three years,** and the places of those of the second class at the expiration of ~~the sixth year~~ **six years,** from the beginning of their term of service; and afterwards the places of senators shall become vacant at the expiration of six years from the beginning of their term of service.

Rotation of senators.
Altered by No. 1, 1907, s. 2.

The election to fill vacant places shall be made ~~in the year at the expiration of which~~ **within one year before** the places are to become vacant.

For the purposes of this section the term of service of a senator shall be taken to begin on the first day of ~~January~~ **July** following the day of his election, except in the cases of the first election and of the election next after any dissolution of the Senate, when it shall be taken to begin on the first day of ~~January~~ **July** preceding the day of his election.

14. Whenever the number of senators for a State is increased or diminished, the Parliament of the Commonwealth may make such provision for the vacating of the places of senators for the State as it deems necessary to maintain regularity in the rotation.[7]

Further provision for rotation.

15.[8] If the place of a senator becomes vacant before the expiration of his term of service, the Houses of Parliament of the State for which he was chosen, sitting and voting together, or, if there is only one House of that Parliament, that House, shall choose a person to hold the place until the expiration of the term. But if the Parliament of the State is not in session when the vacancy is notified, the Governor of the State, with the advice of the Executive Council thereof, may appoint a person to hold the place until the expiration of fourteen days from the beginning of the next session of the Parliament of the State or the expiration of the term, whichever first happens.

Casual vacancies.
Substituted by No., 82, 1977, s. 2.

Where a vacancy has at any time occurred in the place of a senator chosen by the people of a State and, at the time when he was so chosen, he was publicly recognized by a particular political party as being an endorsed candidate of that party and publicly represented himself to be such a candidate, a person chosen or appointed under this section in consequence of that vacancy, or in consequence of that vacancy and a subsequent vacancy or vacancies, shall, unless there is no member of that party available to be chosen or appointed, be a member of that party.

Where—

(a)   in accordance with the last preceding paragraph, a member of a particular political party is chosen or appointed to hold the place of a senator whose place had become vacant; and

(b)   before taking his seat he ceases to be a member of that party (otherwise than by reason of the party having ceased to exist),

he shall be deemed not to have been so chosen or appointed and the vacancy shall be again notified in accordance with section twenty-one of this Constitution.

The name of any senator chosen or appointed under this section shall be certified by the Governor of the State to the Governor-General.

If the place of a senator chosen by the people of a State at the election of senators last held before the commencement of the *Constitution Alteration (Senate Casual Vacancies)* 1977 became vacant before that commencement and, at that commencement, no person chosen by the House or Houses of Parliament of the State, or appointed by the Governor of the State, in consequence of that vacancy, or in consequence of that vacancy and a subsequent vacancy or vacancies, held office, this section applies as if the place of the senator chosen by the people of the State had become vacant after that commencement.

A senator holding office at the commencement of the *Constitution Alteration (Senate Casual Vacancies)* 1977, being a senator appointed by the Governor of a State in consequence of a vacancy that had at any time occurred in the place of a senator chosen by the people of the State, shall be deemed to have been appointed to hold the place until the expiration of fourteen days after the beginning of the next session of the Parliament of the State that commenced or commences after he was appointed and further action under this section shall be taken as if the vacancy in the place of the senator chosen by the people of the State had occurred after that commencement.

Subject to the next succeeding paragraph, a senator holding office at the commencement of the *Constitution Alteration (Senate Casual Vacancies)* 1977 who was chosen by the House or Houses of Parliament of a State in consequence of a vacancy that had at any time occurred in the place of a senator chosen by the people of the State shall be deemed to have been chosen to hold office until the expiration of the term of service of the senator elected by the people of the State.

If, at or before the commencement of the *Constitution Alteration (Senate Casual Vacancies) 1977*, a law to alter the Constitution entitled "*Constitution Alteration (Simultaneous Elections) 1977*" came into operation,⁹ a senator holding office at the commencement of that law who was chosen by the House or Houses of Parliament of a State in consequence of a vacancy that had at any time occurred in the place of a Senator chosen by the people of the State shall be deemed to have been chosen to hold office—

    (a) if the senator elected by the people of the State had a term of service expiring on the thirtieth day of June, One thousand nine hundred and seventy-eight—until the expiration or dissolution of the first House of Representatives to expire or be dissolved after that law came into operation; or

    (b) if the senator elected by the people of the State had a term of service expiring on the thirtieth day of June, One thousand nine hundred and eighty-one—until the expiration or dissolution of the second House of Representatives to expire or be dissolved after that law came into operation or, if there is an earlier dissolution of the Senate, until that dissolution.

16. The qualifications of a senator shall be the same as those of a member of the House of Representatives.

Qualifications of senator.

17. The Senate shall, before proceeding to the despatch of any other business, choose a senator to be the President of the Senate; and as often as the office of President becomes vacant the Senate shall again choose a senator to be the President.

Election of President.

The President shall cease to hold his office if he ceases to be a senator. He may be removed from office by a vote of the Senate, or he may resign his office or his seat by writing addressed to the Governor-General.

18. Before or during any absence of the President, the Senate may choose a senator to perform his duties in his absence.

Absence of President.

19. A senator may, by writing addressed to the President, or to the Governor-General if there is no President or if the President is absent from the Commonwealth, resign his place, which thereupon shall become vacant.

Resignation of senator.

20. The place of a senator shall become vacant if for two consecutive months of any session of the Parliament he, without the permission of the Senate, fails to attend the Senate.

Vacancy by absence.

21. Whenever a vacancy happens in the Senate, the President, or if there is no President or if the President is absent from the Commonwealth the Governor-General, shall notify the same to the Governor of the State in the representation of which the vacancy has happened.

Vacancy to be notified.

Quorum.

22. Until the Parliament otherwise provides, the presence of at least one-third of the whole number of the senators shall be necessary to constitute a meeting of the Senate for the exercise of its powers.

Voting in the Senate.

23. Questions arising in the Senate shall be determined by a majority of votes, and each senator shall have one vote. The President shall in all cases be entitled to a vote; and when the votes are equal the question shall pass in the negative.

Part III. House of Representatives.

PART III.—THE HOUSE OF REPRESENTATIVES.

Constitution of House of Representatives.

24. The House of Representatives shall be composed of members directly chosen by the people of the Commonwealth, and the number of such members shall be, as nearly as practicable, twice the number of the senators.

The number of members chosen in the several States shall be in proportion to the respective numbers of their people, and shall, until the Parliament otherwise provides, be determined, whenever necessary, in the following manner:—

(i.) A quota shall be ascertained by dividing the number of the people of the Commonwealth, as shown by the latest statistics of the Commonwealth, by twice the number of the senators:

(ii.) The number of members to be chosen in each State shall be determined by dividing the number of the people of the State, as shown by the latest statistics of the Commonwealth, by the quota; and if on such division there is a remainder greater than one-half of the quota, one more member shall be chosen in the State.

But notwithstanding anything in this section, five members at least shall be chosen in each Original State.

Provision as to races disqualified from voting.

25. For the purposes of the last section, if by the law of any State all persons of any race are disqualified from voting at elections for the more numerous House of the Parliament of the State, then, in reckoning the number of the people of the State or of the Commonwealth, persons of that race resident in that State shall not be counted.

Representatives in first Parliament.

26. Notwithstanding anything in section twenty-four, the number of members to be chosen in each State at the first election shall be as follows:—

New South Wales . . . . twenty-three;
Victoria . . . . twenty;

Queensland . . . . eight;
South Australia . . . . six;
Tasmania . . . . five;

Provided that if Western Australia is an Original State, the numbers shall be as follows:—

New South Wales . . . . . . twenty-six;
Victoria . . . . twenty-three;
Queensland . . . . nine;
South Australia . . . . . . seven;
Western Australia . . . . . . five;
Tasmania . . . . five.

27. Subject to this Constitution, the Parliament may make laws for increasing or diminishing the number of the members of the House of Representatives.

Alteration of number of members.

28. Every House of Representatives shall continue for three years from the first meeting of the House, and no longer, but may be sooner dissolved by the Governor-General.

Duration of House of Representatives.

29. Until the Parliament of the Commonwealth otherwise provides, the Parliament of any State may make laws[10] for determining the divisions in each State for which members of the House of Representatives may be chosen, and the number of members to be chosen for each division. A division shall not be formed out of parts of different States.

Electoral divisions.

In the absence of other provision, each State shall be one electorate.

30. Until the Parliament otherwise provides, the qualification of electors of members of the House of Representatives shall be in each State that which is prescribed by the law of the State as the qualification of electors of the more numerous House of Parliament of the State; but in the choosing of members each elector shall vote only once.

Qualification of electors.

31. Until the Parliament otherwise provides, but subject to this Constitution, the laws in force in each State for the time being relating to elections for the more numerous House of the Parliament of the State shall, as nearly as practicable, apply to elections in the State of members of the House of Representatives.

Application of State laws.

32. The Governor-General in Council may cause writs to be issued for general elections of members of the House of Representatives.

Writs for general election.

After the first general election, the writs shall be issued within ten days from the expiry of a House of Representatives or from the proclamation of a dissolution thereof.

Writs for vacancies.   **33.** Whenever a vacancy happens in the House of Representatives, the Speaker shall issue his writ for the election of a new member, or if there is no Speaker or if he is absent from the Commonwealth the Governor-General in Council may issue the writ.

Qualifications of members.   **34.** Until the Parliament otherwise provides, the qualifications of a member of the House of Representatives shall be as follows:—

     (i.) He must be of the full age of twenty-one years, and must be an elector entitled to vote at the election of members of the House of Representatives, or a person qualified to become such elector, and must have been for three years at the least a resident within the limits of the Commonwealth as existing at the time when he is chosen:

     (ii.) He must be a subject of the Queen, either natural-born or for at least five years naturalized under a law of the United Kingdom, or of a Colony which has become or becomes a State, or of the Commonwealth, or of a State.

Election of Speaker.   **35.** The House of Representatives shall, before proceeding to the despatch of any other business, choose a member to be the Speaker of the House, and as often as the office of Speaker becomes vacant the House shall again choose a member to be the Speaker.

The Speaker shall cease to hold his office if he ceases to be a member. He may be removed from office by a vote of the House, or he may resign his office or his seat by writing addressed to the Governor-General.

Absence of Speaker.   **36.** Before or during any absence of the Speaker, the House of Representatives may choose a member to perform his duties in his absence.

Resignation of member.   **37.** A member may by writing addressed to the Speaker, or to the Governor-General if there is no Speaker or if the Speaker is absent from the Commonwealth, resign his place, which thereupon shall become vacant.

Vacancy by absence.   **38.** The place of a member shall become vacant if for two consecutive months of any session of the Parliament he, without the permission of the House, fails to attend the House.

Quorum.   **39.** Until the Parliament otherwise provides, the presence of at least one-third of the whole number of the members of the House of Representatives shall be necessary to constitute a meeting of the House for the exercise of its powers.

Voting in House of Representatives.   **40.** Questions arising in the House of Representatives shall be determined by a majority of votes other than that of the Speaker. The Speaker shall not vote unless the numbers are equal, and then he shall have a casting vote.

PART IV.—BOTH HOUSES OF THE PARLIAMENT.

41. No adult person who has or acquires a right to vote at elections for the more numerous House of the Parliament of a State shall, while the right continues, be prevented by any law of the Commonwealth from voting at elections for either House of the Parliament of the Commonwealth.

42. Every senator and every member of the House of Representatives shall before taking his seat make and subscribe before the Governor-General, or some person authorised by him, an oath or affirmation of allegiance in the form set forth in the schedule to this Constitution.

43. A member of either House of the Parliament shall be incapable of being chosen or of sitting as a member of the other House.

44. Any person who—

- (i.) Is under any acknowledgment of allegiance, obedience, or adherence to a foreign power, or is a subject or a citizen or entitled to the rights or privileges of a subject or a citizen of a foreign power: or
- (ii.) Is attainted of treason, or has been convicted and is under sentence, or subject to be sentenced, for any offence punishable under the law of the Commonwealth or of a State by imprisonment for one year or longer: or
- (iii.) Is an undischarged bankrupt or insolvent: or
- (iv.) Holds any office of profit under the Crown, or any pension payable during the pleasure of the Crown out of any of the revenues of the Commonwealth: or
- (v.) Has any direct or indirect pecuniary interest in any agreement with the Public Service of the Commonwealth otherwise than as a member and in common with the other members of an incorporated company consisting of more than twenty-five persons:

shall be incapable of being chosen or of sitting as a senator or a member of the House of Representatives.

But sub-section iv. does not apply to the office of any of the Queen's Ministers of State for the Commonwealth, or of any of the Queen's Ministers for a State, or to the receipt of pay, half pay, or a pension, by any person as an officer or member of the Queen's navy or army, or to the receipt of pay as an officer or member of the naval or military forces of the Commonwealth by any person whose services are not wholly employed by the Commonwealth.

Vacancy on happening of disqualification.

45. If a senator or member of the House of Representatives—

(i.) Becomes subject to any of the disabilities mentioned in the last preceding section: or

(ii.) Takes the benefit, whether by assignment, composition, or otherwise, of any law relating to bankrupt or insolvent debtors: or

(iii.) Directly or indirectly takes or agrees to take any fee or honorarium for services rendered to the Commonwealth, or for services rendered in the Parliament to any person or State:

his place shall thereupon become vacant.

Penalty for sitting when disqualified.

46. Until the Parliament otherwise provides, any person declared by this Constitution to be incapable of sitting as a senator or as a member of the House of Representatives shall, for every day on which he so sits, be liable to pay the sum of one hundred pounds to any person who sues for it in any court of competent jurisdiction.

Disputed elections.

47. Until the Parliament otherwise provides, any question respecting the qualification of a senator or of a member of the House of Representatives, or respecting a vacancy in either House of the Parliament, and any question of a disputed election to either House, shall be determined by the House in which the question arises.

Allowance to members.

48. Until the Parliament otherwise provides, each senator and each member of the House of Representatives shall receive an allowance of four hundred pounds a year, to be reckoned from the day on which he takes his seat.

Privileges, &c. of Houses.

49. The powers, privileges, and immunities of the Senate and of the House of Representatives, and of the members and the committees of each House, shall be such as are declared by the Parliament, and until declared shall be those of the Commons House of Parliament of the United Kingdom, and of its members and committees, at the establishment of the Commonwealth.

Rules and orders.

50. Each House of the Parliament may make rules and orders with respect to—

(i.) The mode in which its powers, privileges, and immunities may be exercised and upheld:

(ii.) The order and conduct of its business and proceedings either separately or jointly with the other House.

PART V.—POWERS OF THE PARLIAMENT.

51. The Parliament shall, subject to this Constitution, have power[11] to make laws for the peace, order, and good government of the Commonwealth with respect to:—

(i.) Trade and commerce with other countries, and among the States:

(ii.) Taxation; but so as not to discriminate between States or parts of States:

(iii.) Bounties on the production or export of goods, but so that such bounties shall be uniform throughout the Commonwealth:

(iv.) Borrowing money on the public credit of the Commonwealth:

(v.) Postal, telegraphic, telephonic, and other like services:

(vi.) The naval and military defence of the Commonwealth and of the several States, and the control of the forces to execute and maintain the laws of the Commonwealth:

(vii.) Lighthouses, lightships, beacons and buoys:

(viii.) Astronomical and meteorological observations:

(ix.) Quarantine:

(x.) Fisheries in Australian waters beyond territorial limits:

(xi.) Census and statistics:

(xii.) Currency, coinage, and legal tender:

(xiii.) Banking, other than State banking; also State banking extending beyond the limits of the State concerned, the incorporation of banks, and the issue of paper money:

(xiv.) Insurance, other than State insurance; also State insurance extending beyond the limits of the State concerned:

(xv.) Weights and measures:

(xvi.) Bills of exchange and promissory notes:

(xvii.) Bankruptcy and insolvency:

(xviii.) Copyrights, patents of inventions and designs, and trade marks:

(xix.) Naturalization and aliens:

(xx.) Foreign corporations, and trading or financial corporations formed within the limits of the Commonwealth:

(xxi.) Marriage:

(xxii.) Divorce and matrimonial causes; and in relation thereto, parental rights, and the custody and guardianship of infants:

(xxiii.) Invalid and old-age pensions:

Inserted by
No. 81. 1946,
s. 2.

(xxiiiA.) The provision of maternity allowances, widows' pensions, child endowment, unemployment, pharmaceutical, sickness and hospital benefits, medical and dental services (but not so as to authorize any form of civil conscription), benefits to students and family allowances:

(xxiv.) The service and execution throughout the Commonwealth of the civil and criminal process and the judgments of the courts of the States:

(xxv.) The recognition throughout the Commonwealth of the laws, the public Acts and records, and the judicial proceedings of the States:

Altered by
No. 55. 1967.
s. 2.

(xxvi.) The people of any race, ~~other than the aboriginal race in any State,~~ for whom it is deemed necessary to make special laws:

(xxvii.) Immigration and emigration:

(xxviii.) The influx of criminals:

(xxix.) External affairs:

(xxx.) The relations of the Commonwealth with the islands of the Pacific:

(xxxi.) The acquisition of property on just terms from any State or person for any purpose in respect of which the Parliament has power to make laws:

(xxxii.) The control of railways with respect to transport for the naval and military purposes of the Commonwealth:

(xxxiii.) The acquisition, with the consent of a State, of any railways of the State on terms arranged between the Commonwealth and the State:

(xxxiv.) Railway construction and extension in any State with the consent of that State:

(xxxv.) Conciliation and arbitration for the prevention and settlement of industrial disputes extending beyond the limits of any one State:

(xxxvi.) Matters in respect of which this Constitution makes provision until the Parliament otherwise provides:

(xxxvii.) Matters referred to the Parliament of the Commonwealth by the Parliament or Parliaments of any State or States,[12] but so that the law shall extend only to States by whose Parliaments the matter is referred, or which afterwards adopt the law:

(xxxviii.) The exercise within the Commonwealth, at the request or with the concurrence of the Parliaments of all the States directly concerned, of any power which can at the establishment of this Constitution be exercised only by the Parliament of the United Kingdom or by the Federal Council of Australasia:

(xxxix.) Matters incidental to the execution of any power vested by this Constitution in the Parliament or in either House thereof, or in the Government of the Commonwealth, or in the Federal Judicature, or in any department or officer of the Commonwealth.

52. The Parliament shall, subject to this Constitution, have exclusive power to make laws for the peace, order, and good government of the Commonwealth with respect to— *Exclusive powers of the Parliament.*

(i.) The seat of government of the Commonwealth, and all places acquired by the Commonwealth for public purposes:

(ii.) Matters relating to any department of the public service the control of which is by this Constitution transferred to the Executive Government of the Commonwealth:

(iii.) Other matters declared by this Constitution to be within the exclusive power of the Parliament.

53. Proposed laws appropriating revenue or moneys, or imposing taxation, shall not originate in the Senate. But a proposed law shall not be taken to appropriate revenue or moneys, or to impose taxation, by reason only of its containing provisions for the imposition or appropriation of fines or other pecuniary penalties, or for the demand or payment or appropriation of fees for licences, or fees for services under the proposed law. *Powers of the Houses in respect of legislation.*

The Senate may not amend proposed laws imposing taxation, or proposed laws appropriating revenue or moneys for the ordinary annual services of the Government.

The Senate may not amend any proposed law so as to increase any proposed charge or burden on the people.

The Senate may at any stage return to the House of Representatives any proposed law which the Senate may not amend, requesting, by message, the omission or amendment of any items or provisions therein. And the House of Representatives may, if it thinks fit, make any of such omissions or amendments, with or without modifications.

Except as provided in this section, the Senate shall have equal power with the House of Representatives in respect of all proposed laws.

54. The proposed law which appropriates revenue or moneys for the ordinary annual services of the Government shall deal only with such appropriation. *Appropriation Bills.*

55. Laws imposing taxation shall deal only with the imposition of taxation, and any provision therein dealing with any other matter shall be of no effect. *Tax Bill.*

Laws imposing taxation, except laws imposing duties of customs or of excise, shall deal with one subject of taxation only; but laws imposing duties of customs shall deal with duties of customs only, and laws imposing duties of excise shall deal with duties of excise only.

56. A vote, resolution, or proposed law for the appropriation of revenue or moneys shall not be passed unless the purpose of the appropriation has in the same session been recommended by message of the Governor-General to the House in which the proposal originated.

57. If the House of Representatives passes any proposed law, and the Senate rejects or fails to pass it, or passes it with amendments to which the House of Representatives will not agree, and if after an interval of three months the House of Representatives, in the same or the next session, again passes the proposed law with or without any amendments which have been made, suggested, or agreed to by the Senate, and the Senate rejects or fails to pass it, or passes it with amendments to which the House of Representatives will not agree, the Governor-General may dissolve the Senate and the House of Representatives simultaneously. But such dissolution shall not take place within six months before the date of the expiry of the House of Representatives by effluxion of time.

If after such dissolution the House of Representatives again passes the proposed law, with or without any amendments which have been made, suggested, or agreed to by the Senate, and the Senate rejects or fails to pass it. or passes it with amendments to which the House of Representatives will not agree, the Governor-General may convene a joint sitting of the members of the Senate and of the House of Representatives.

The members present at the joint sitting may deliberate and shall vote together upon the proposed law as last proposed by the House of Representatives, and upon amendments, if any, which have been made therein by one House and not agreed to by the other, and any such amendments which are affirmed by an absolute majority of the total number of the members of the Senate and House of Representatives shall be taken to have been carried, and if the proposed law, with the amendments, if any, so carried is affirmed by an absolute majority of the total number of the members of the Senate and House of Representatives, it shall be taken to have been duly passed by both Houses of the Parliament, and shall be presented to the Governor-General for the Queen's assent.

58. When a proposed law passed by both Houses of the Parliament is presented to the Governor-General for the Queen's assent, he shall declare, according to his discretion, but subject to this Constitution, that he assents in the Queen's name, or that he withholds assent, or that he reserves the law for the Queen's pleasure.

The Governor-General may return to the house in which it originated any proposed law so presented to him, and may transmit therewith any amendments which he may recommend, and the Houses may deal with the recommendation.

59. The Queen may disallow any law within one year from the Governor-General's assent, and such disallowance on being made known by the Governor-General by speech or message to each of the Houses of the Parliament, or by Proclamation, shall annul the law from the day when the disallowance is so made known.

60. A proposed law reserved for the Queen's pleasure shall not have any force unless and until within two years from the day on which it was presented to the Governor-General for the Queen's assent the Governor-General makes known, by speech or message to each of the Houses of the Parliament, or by Proclamation, that it has received the Queen's assent.

CHAPTER II.

THE EXECUTIVE GOVERNMENT.

61. The executive power of the Commonwealth is vested in the Queen and is exercisable by the Governor-General as the Queen's representative, and extends to the execution and maintenance of this Constitution, and of the laws of the Commonwealth.

62. There shall be a Federal Executive Council to advise the Governor-General in the government of the Commonwealth, and the members of the Council shall be chosen and summoned by the Governor-General and sworn as Executive Councillors, and shall hold office during his pleasure.

63. The provisions of this Constitution referring to the Governor-General in Council shall be construed as referring to the Governor-General acting with the advice of the Federal Executive Council.

64. The Governor-General may appoint officers to administer such departments of State of the Commonwealth as the Governor-General in Council may establish.

Such officers shall hold office during the pleasure of the Governor-General. They shall be members of the Federal Executive Council, and shall be the Queen's Ministers of State for the Commonwealth.

Ministers to sit in Parliament.   After the first general election no Minister of State shall hold office for a longer period than three months unless he is or becomes a senator or a member of the House of Representatives.

Number of Ministers.   **65.** Until the Parliament otherwise provides, the Ministers of State shall not exceed seven in number, and shall hold such offices as the Parliament prescribes, or, in the absence of provision, as the Governor-General directs.

Salaries of Ministers.   **66.** There shall be payable to the Queen, out of the Consolidated Revenue Fund of the Commonwealth, for the salaries of the Ministers of State, an annual sum which, until the Parliament otherwise provides, shall not exceed twelve thousand pounds a year.

Appointment of civil servants.   **67.** Until the Parliament otherwise provides, the appointment and removal of all other officers of the Executive Government of the Commonwealth shall be vested in the Governor-General in Council, unless the appointment is delegated by the Governor-General in Council or by a law of the Commonwealth to some other authority.

Command of naval and military forces.   **68.** The command in chief of the naval and military forces of the Commonwealth is vested in the Governor-General as the Queen's representative.

Transfer of certain departments.   **69.** On a date or dates to be proclaimed by the Governor-General after the establishment of the Commonwealth the following departments of the public service in each State shall become transferred to the Commonwealth: —

> Posts, telegraphs, and telephones:
> Naval and military defence:
> Lighthouses, lightships, beacons, and buoys:
> Quarantine.

But the departments of customs and of excise in each State shall become transferred to the Commonwealth on its establishment.

Certain powers of Governors to vest in Governor-General.   **70.** In respect of matters which, under this Constitution, pass to the Executive Government of the Commonwealth, all powers and functions which at the establishment of the Commonwealth are vested in the Governor of a Colony, or in the Governor of a Colony with the advice of his Executive Council, or in any authority of a Colony, shall vest in the Governor-General, or in the Governor-General in Council, or in the authority exercising similar powers under the Commonwealth, as the case requires.

CHAPTER III.

THE JUDICATURE.

71. The judicial power of the Commonwealth shall be vested in a Federal Supreme Court, to be called the High Court of Australia, and in such other federal courts as the Parliament creates, and in such other courts as it invests with federal jurisdiction. The High Court shall consist of a Chief Justice, and so many other Justices, not less than two, as the Parliament prescribes.

Judicial power and Courts.

72. The Justices of the High Court and of the other courts created by the Parliament—

Judges' appointment, tenure and remuneration.

    (i.)   Shall be appointed by the Governor-General in Council:

    (ii.) Shall not be removed except by the Governor-General in Council, on an address from both Houses of the Parliament in the same session, praying for such removal on the ground of proved misbehaviour or incapacity:

    (iii.) Shall receive such remuneration as the Parliament may fix; but the remuneration shall not be diminished during their continuance in office.

The appointment of a Justice of the High Court shall be for a term expiring upon his attaining the age of seventy years, and a person shall not be appointed as a Justice of the High Court if he has attained that age.

Paragraph added by No. 83, 1977, s. 2.

The appointment of a Justice of a court created by the Parliament shall be for a term expiring upon his attaining the age that is, at the time of his appointment, the maximum age for Justices of that court and a person shall not be appointed as a Justice of such a court if he has attained the age that is for the time being the maximum age for Justices of that court.

Paragraph added by No. 83, 1977, s. 2.

Subject to this section, the maximum age for Justices of any court created by the Parliament is seventy years.

Paragraph added by No. 83, 1977, s. 2.

The Parliament may make a law fixing an age that is less than seventy years as the maximum age for Justices of a court created by the Parliament and may at any time repeal or amend such a law, but any such repeal or amendment does not affect the term of office of a Justice under an appointment made before the repeal or amendment.

Paragraph added by No. 83, 1977, s. 2.

A Justice of the High Court or of a court created by the Parliament may resign his office by writing under his hand delivered to the Governor-General.

Paragraph added by No. 83, 1977, s. 2.

Nothing in the provisions added to this section by the *Constitution Alteration (Retirement of Judges)* 1977 affects the continuance of a person in office as a Justice of a court under an appointment made before the commencement of those provisions.

Paragraph added by No. 83, 1977, s. 2.

Paragraph
added by No. 83.
1977, s. 2.
A reference in this section to the appointment of a Justice of the High Court or of a court created by the Parliament shall be read as including a reference to the appointment of a person who holds office as a Justice of the High Court or of a court created by the Parliament to another office of Justice of the same court having a different status or designation.

**Appellate
jurisdiction
of High
Court.**
73. The High Court shall have jurisdiction, with such exceptions and subject to such regulations as the Parliament prescribes, to hear and determine appeals from all judgments, decrees, orders, and sentences—

(i.)   Of any Justice or Justices exercising the original jurisdiction of the High Court:

(ii.)   Of any other federal court, or court exercising federal jurisdiction; or of the Supreme Court of any State, or of any other court of any State from which at the establishment of the Commonwealth an appeal lies to the Queen in Council:

(iii.)   Of the Inter-State Commission, but as to questions of law only:

and the judgment of the High Court in all such cases shall be final and conclusive.

But no exception or regulation prescribed by the Parliament shall prevent the High Court from hearing and determining any appeal from the Supreme Court of a State in any matter in which at the establishment of the Commonwealth an appeal lies from such Supreme Court to the Queen in Council.

Until the Parliament otherwise provides, the conditions of and restrictions on appeals to the Queen in Council from the Supreme Courts of the several States shall be applicable to appeals from them to the High Court.

**Appeal to
Queen in
Council.**
74. No appeal shall be permitted to the Queen in Council from a decision of the High Court upon any question, howsoever arising, as to the limits inter se of the Constitutional powers of the Commonwealth and those of any State or States, or as to the limits inter se of the Constitutional powers of any two or more States, unless the High Court shall certify that the question is one which ought to be determined by Her Majesty in Council.

The High Court may so certify if satisfied that for any special reason the certificate should be granted, and thereupon an appeal shall lie to Her Majesty in Council on the question without further leave.

Except as provided in this section, this Constitution shall not impair any right which the Queen may be pleased to exercise by virtue of Her Royal prerogative to grant special leave of appeal from the High Court to Her Majesty in Council. The Parliament may make laws limiting the matters in which such leave may be asked,[13] but proposed laws containing any such limitation shall be reserved by the Governor-General for Her Majesty's pleasure.

75. In all matters— *original jurisdiction*

(i.) Arising under any treaty:

(ii.) Affecting consuls or other representatives of other countries:

(iii.) In which the Commonwealth, or a person suing or being sued on behalf of the Commonwealth, is a party:

(iv.) Between States, or between residents of different States, or between a State and a resident of another State:

(v.) In which a writ of Mandamus or prohibition or an injunction is sought against an officer of the Commonwealth:

the High Court shall have original jurisdiction.

Original jurisdiction of High Court.

76. The Parliament may make laws conferring original jurisdiction on the High Court in any matter—

(i.) Arising under this Constitution, or involving its interpretation:

(ii.) Arising under any laws made by the Parliament:

(iii.) Of Admiralty and maritime jurisdiction:

(iv.) Relating to the same subject-matter claimed under the laws of different States.

Additional original jurisdiction.

77. With respect to any of the matters mentioned in the last two sections the Parliament may make laws—

(i.) Defining the jurisdiction of any federal court other than the High Court:

(ii.) Defining the extent to which the jurisdiction of any federal court shall be exclusive of that which belongs to or is invested in the courts of the States:

(iii.) Investing any court of a State with federal jurisdiction.

Power to define jurisdiction.

78. The Parliament may make laws conferring rights to proceed against the Commonwealth or a State in respect of matters within the limits of the judicial power.

Proceedings against Commonwealth or State.

79. The federal jurisdiction of any court may be exercised by such number of judges as the Parliament prescribes.

Number of judges.

80. The trial on indictment of any offence against any law of the Commonwealth shall be by jury, and every such trial shall be held in the State where the offence was committed, and if the offence was not committed within any State the trial shall be held at such place or places as the Parliament prescribes.

Trial by jury.

_____

č 71–80

CHAPTER IV.

FINANCE AND TRADE.

Consolidated
Revenue
Fund.

81. All revenues or moneys raised or received by the Executive Government of the Commonwealth shall form one Consolidated Revenue Fund, to be appropriated for the purposes of the Commonwealth in the manner and subject to the charges and liabilities imposed by this Constitution.

Expenditure
charged
thereon.

82. The costs, charges, and expenses incident to the collection, management, and receipt of the Consolidated Revenue Fund shall form the first charge thereon; and the revenue of the Commonwealth shall in the first instance be applied to the payment of the expenditure of the Commonwealth.

Money to be
appropriated
by law.

83. No money shall be drawn from the Treasury of the Commonwealth except under appropriation made by law.

But until the expiration of one month after the first meeting of the Parliament the Governor-General in Council may draw from the Treasury and expend such moneys as may be necessary for the maintenance of any department transferred to the Commonwealth and for the holding of the first elections for the Parliament.

Transfer of
officers.

84. When any department of the public service of a State becomes transferred to the Commonwealth, all officers of the department shall become subject to the control of the Executive Government of the Commonwealth.

Any such officer who is not retained in the service of the Commonwealth shall, unless he is appointed to some other office of equal emolument in the public service of the State, be entitled to receive from the State any pension, gratuity, or other compensation, payable under the law of the State on the abolition of his office.

Any such officer who is retained in the service of the Commonwealth shall preserve all his existing and accruing rights, and shall be entitled to retire from office at the time, and on the pension or retiring allowance, which would be permitted by the law of the State if his service with the Commonwealth were a continuation of his service with the State. Such pension or retiring allowance shall be paid to him by the Commonwealth; but the State shall pay to the Commonwealth a part thereof, to be calculated on the proportion which his term of service with the State bears to his whole term of service, and for the purpose of the calculation his salary shall be taken to be that paid to him by the State at the time of the transfer.

Any officer who is, at the establishment of the Commonwealth, in the public service of a State, and who is, by consent of the Governor of the State with the advice of the Executive Council thereof, transferred to the public service of the Commonwealth, shall have the same rights as if he had been an officer of a department transferred to the Commonwealth and were retained in the service of the Commonwealth.

85. When any department of the public service of a State is transfer-ed to the Commonwealth— Transfer of property of State.

> (i.) All property of the State of any kind, used exclusively in con-nexion with the department, shall become vested in the Com-monwealth; but, in the case of the departments controlling cus-toms and excise and bounties, for such time only as the Gover-nor-General in Council may declare to be necessary:

> (ii.) The Commonwealth may acquire any property of the State, of any kind used, but not exclusively used in connexion with the department; the value thereof shall, if no agreement can be made, be ascertained in, as nearly as may be, the manner in which the value of land, or of an interest in land, taken by the State for public purposes is ascertained under the law of the State in force at the establishment of the Commonwealth:

> (iii.) The Commonwealth shall compensate the State for the value of any property passing to the Commonwealth under this section; if no agreement can be made as to the mode of compensation, it shall be determined under laws to be made by the Parliament:

> (iv.) The Commonwealth shall, at the date of the transfer, assume the current obligations of the State in respect of the department transferred.

86. On the establishment of the Commonwealth, the collection and control of duties of customs and of excise, and the control of the payment of bounties, shall pass to the Executive Government of the Common-wealth.

87. During a period of ten years after the establishment of the Com-monwealth and thereafter until the Parliament otherwise provides, of the net revenue of the Commonwealth from duties of customs and of excise not more than one-fourth shall be applied annually by the Com-monwealth towards its expenditure.

The balance shall, in accordance with this Constitution, be paid to the several States, or applied towards the payment of interest on debts of the several States taken over by the Commonwealth.

88. Uniform duties of customs shall be imposed within two years after the establishment of the Commonwealth. Uniform duties of customs.

Payment to States before uniform duties.

89. Until the imposition of uniform duties of customs—

(i.) The Commonwealth shall credit to each State the revenues collected therein by the Commonwealth.

(ii.) The Commonwealth shall debit to each State—

   (*a*) The expenditure therein of the Commonwealth incurred solely for the maintenance or continuance, as at the time of transfer, of any department transferred from the State to the Commonwealth;

   (*b*) The proportion of the State, according to the number of its people, in the other expenditure of the Commonwealth.

(iii.) The Commonwealth shall pay to each State month by month the balance (if any) in favour of the State.

Exclusive power over customs, excise, and bounties.

90. On the imposition of uniform duties of customs the power of the Parliament to impose duties of customs and of excise, and to grant bounties on the production or export of goods, shall become exclusive.

On the imposition of uniform duties of customs all laws of the several States imposing duties of customs or of excise, or offering bounties on the production or export of goods, shall cease to have effect, but any grant of or agreement for any such bounty lawfully made by or under the authority of the Government of any State shall be taken to be good if made before the thirtieth day of June, one thousand eight hundred and ninety-eight, and not otherwise.

Exceptions as to bounties.

91. Nothing in this Constitution prohibits a State from granting any aid to or bounty on mining for gold, silver, or other metals, nor from granting, with the consent of both Houses of the Parliament of the Commonwealth expressed by resolution, any aid to or bounty on the production or export of goods.

Trade within the Commonwealth to be free.

92. On the imposition of uniform duties of customs, trade, commerce, and intercourse among the States, whether by means of internal carriage or ocean navigation, shall be absolutely free.

But notwithstanding anything in this Constitution, goods imported before the imposition of uniform duties of customs into any State, or into any Colony which, whilst the goods remain therein, becomes a State, shall, on thence passing into another State within two years after the imposition of such duties, be liable to any duty chargeable on the importation of such goods into the Commonwealth, less any duty paid in respect of the goods on their importation.

93. During the first five years after the imposition of uniform duties of customs, and thereafter until the Parliament otherwise provides—

> (i.) The duties of customs chargeable on goods imported into a State and afterwards passing into another State for consumption, and the duties of excise paid on goods produced or manufactured in a State and afterwards passing into another State for consumption, shall be taken to have been collected not in the former but in the latter State:

> (ii.) Subject to the last subsection, the Commonwealth shall credit revenue, debit expenditure, and pay balances to the several States as prescribed for the period preceding the imposition of uniform duties of customs.

94. After five years from the imposition of uniform duties of customs, the Parliament may provide, on such basis as it deems fair, for the monthly payment to the several States of all surplus revenue of the Commonwealth.

95. Notwithstanding anything in this Constitution, the Parliament of the State of Western Australia, if that State be an Original State, may, during the first five years after the imposition of uniform duties of customs, impose duties of customs on goods passing into that State and not originally imported from beyond the limits of the Commonwealth; and such duties shall be collected by the Commonwealth.

But any duty so imposed on any goods shall not exceed during the first of such years the duty chargeable on the goods under the law of Western Australia in force at the imposition of uniform duties, and shall not exceed during the second, third, fourth, and fifth of such years respectively, four-fifths, three-fifths, two-fifths, and one-fifth of such latter duty, and all duties imposed under this section shall cease at the expiration of the fifth year after the imposition of uniform duties.

If at any time during the five years the duty on any goods under this section is higher than the duty imposed by the Commonwealth on the importation of the like goods, then such higher duty shall be collected on the goods when imported into Western Australia from beyond the limits of the Commonwealth.

96. During a period of ten years after the establishment of the Commonwealth and thereafter until the Parliament otherwise provides, the Parliament may grant financial assistance to any State on such terms and conditions as the Parliament thinks fit.

97. Until the Parliament otherwise provides, the laws in force in any Colony which has become or becomes a State with respect to the receipt of revenue and the expenditure of money on account of the Government of the Colony, and the review and audit of such receipt and expenditure, shall apply to the receipt of revenue and the expenditure of money on account of the Commonwealth in the State in the same manner as if the Commonwealth, or the Government or an officer of the Commonwealth, were mentioned whenever the Colony, or the Government or an officer of the Colony, is mentioned.

Trade and commerce includes navigation and State railways.

98. The power of the Parliament to make laws with respect to trade and commerce extends to navigation and shipping, and to railways the property of any State.

Commonwealth not to give preference.

99. The Commonwealth shall not, by any law or regulation of trade, commerce, or revenue, give preference to one State or any part thereof over another State or any part thereof.

Nor abridge right to use water.

100. The Commonwealth shall not, by any law or regulation of trade or commerce, abridge the right of a State or of the residents therein to the reasonable use of the waters of rivers for conservation or irrigation.

Inter-State Commission.

101. There shall be an Inter-State Commission, with such powers of adjudication and administration as the Parliament deems necessary for the execution and maintenance, within the Commonwealth, of the provisions of this Constitution relating to trade and commerce, and of all laws made thereunder.

Parliament may forbid preferences by State.

102. The Parliament may by any law with respect to trade or commerce forbid, as to railways, any preference or discrimination by any State, or by any authority constituted under a State, if such preference or discrimination is undue and unreasonable, or unjust to any State; due regard being had to the financial responsibilities incurred by any State in connexion with the construction and maintenance of its railways. But no preference or discrimination shall, within the meaning of this section, be taken to be undue and unreasonable, or unjust to any State, unless so adjudged by the Inter-State Commission.

Commissioners' appointment, tenure, and remuneration.

103. The members of the Inter-State Commission—

(i.) Shall be appointed by the Governor-General in Council:

(ii.) Shall hold office for seven years, but may be removed within that time by the Governor-General in Council, on an address from both Houses of the Parliament in the same session praying for such removal on the ground of proved misbehaviour or incapacity:

(iii.) Shall receive such remuneration as the Parliament may fix; but such remuneration shall not be diminished during their continuance in office.

Saving of certain rates.

104. Nothing in this Constitution shall render unlawful any rate for the carriage of goods upon a railway, the property of a State, if the rate is deemed by the Inter-State Commission to be necessary for the development of the territory of the State, and if the rate applies equally to goods within the State and to goods passing into the State from other States.

105. The Parliament may take over from the States their public debts as existing at the establishment of the Commonwealth, or a proportion thereof according to the respective numbers of their people as shown by the latest statistics of the Commonwealth, and may convert, renew, or consolidate such debts, or any part thereof; and the States shall indemnify the Commonwealth in respect of the debts taken over, and thereafter the interest payable in respect of the debts shall be deducted and retained from the portions of the surplus revenue of the Commonwealth payable to the several States, or if such surplus is insufficient, or if there is no surplus, then the deficiency or the whole amount shall be paid by the several States.

Taking over public debts of States.

Altered by No.3, 1910, s. 2.

105A.—(1.) The Commonwealth may make agreements with the States with respect to the public debts of the States, including—

(*a*)   the taking over of such debts by the Commonwealth;

(*b*)   the management of such debts;

(*c*)   the payment of interest and the provision and management of sinking funds in respect of such debts;

(*d*)   the consolidation, renewal, conversion, and redemption of such debts;

(*e*)   the indemnification of the Commonwealth by the States in respect of debts taken over by the Commonwealth; and

(*f*)   the borrowing of money by the States or by the Commonwealth, or by the Commonwealth for the States.

Agreements with respect to State debts.

Inserted by No. 1, 1929, s. 2.

(2.) The Parliament may make laws for validating any such agreement made before the commencement of this section.

(3.) The Parliament may make laws for the carrying out by the parties thereto of any such agreement.

(4.) Any such agreement may be varied or rescinded by the parties thereto.

(5.) Every such agreement and any such variation thereof shall be binding upon the Commonwealth and the States parties thereto notwithstanding anything contained in this Constitution or the Constitution of the several States or in any law of the Parliament of the Commonwealth or of any State.

(6.) The powers conferred by this section shall not be construed as being limited in any way by the provisions of section one hundred and five of this Constitution.

———

CHAPTER V.

THE STATES.

Saving of
Constitutions.

106. The Constitution of each State of the Commonwealth shall, subject to this Constitution, continue as at the establishment of the Commonwealth, or as at the admission or establishment of the State, as the case may be, until altered in accordance with the Constitution of the State.

Saving of
Power of
State
Parliaments.

107. Every power of the Parliament of a Colony which has become or becomes a State, shall, unless it is by this Constitution exclusively vested in the Parliament of the Commonwealth or withdrawn from the Parliament of the State, continue as at the establishment of the Commonwealth, or as at the admission or establishment of the State, as the case may be.

Saving of
State laws.

108. Every law in force in a Colony which has become or becomes a State, and relating to any matter within the powers of the Parliament of the Commonwealth, shall, subject to this Constitution, continue in force in the State; and, until provision is made in that behalf by the Parliament of the Commonwealth, the Parliament of the State shall have such powers of alteration and of repeal in respect of any such law as the Parliament of the Colony had until the Colony became a State.

Inconsistency
of laws.

109. When a law of a State is inconsistent with a law of the Commonwealth, the latter shall prevail, and the former shall, to the extent of the inconsistency, be invalid.

Provisions
referring to
Governor.

110. The provisions of this Constitution relating to the Governor of a State extend and apply to the Governor for the time being of the State, or other chief executive officer or administrator of the government of the State.

States may
surrender
territory.

111. The Parliament of a State may surrender any part of the State to the Commonwealth; and upon such surrender, and the acceptance thereof by the Commonwealth, such part of the State shall become subject to the exclusive jurisdiction of the Commonwealth.

States may
levy charges
for
inspection
laws.

112. After uniform duties of customs have been imposed, a State may levy on imports or exports, or on goods passing into or out of the State, such charges as may be necessary for executing the inspection laws of the State; but the net produce of all charges so levied shall be for the use of the Commonwealth; and any such inspection laws may be annulled by the Parliament of the Commonwealth.

Intoxicating
liquids.

113. All fermented, distilled, or other intoxicating liquids passing into any State or remaining therein for use, consumption, sale, or storage, shall be subject to the laws of the State as if such liquids had been produced in the State.

114. A State shall not, without the consent of the Parliament of the Commonwealth, raise or maintain any naval or military force, or impose any tax on property of any kind belonging to the Commonwealth, nor shall the Commonwealth impose any tax on property of any kind belonging to a State.

States may not raise forces. Taxation of property of Commonwealth or State.

115. A State shall not coin money, nor make anything but gold and silver coin a legal tender in payment of debts.

States not to coin money.

116. The Commonwealth shall not make any law for establishing any religion, or for imposing any religious observance, or for prohibiting the free exercise of any religion, and no religious test shall be required as a qualification for any office or public trust under the Commonwealth.

Commonwealth not to legislate in respect of religion.

117. A subject of the Queen, resident in any State, shall not be subject in any other State to any disability or discrimination which would not be equally applicable to him if he were a subject of the Queen resident in such other State.

Rights of residents in States.

118. Full faith and credit shall be given, throughout the Commonwealth to the laws, the public Acts and records, and the judicial proceedings of every State.

Recognition of laws, &c. of States.

119. The Commonwealth shall protect every State against invasion and, on the application of the Executive Government of the State, against domestic violence.

Protection of States from invasion and violence.

120. Every State shall make provision for the detention in its prisons of persons accused or convicted of offences against the laws of the Commonwealth, and for the punishment of persons convicted of such offences, and the Parliament of the Commonwealth may make laws to give effect to this provision.

Custody of offenders against laws of the Commonwealth.

CHAPTER VI.

NEW STATES.

Chap. VI. New States.

121. The Parliament may admit to the Commonwealth or establish new States, and may upon such admission or establishment make or impose such terms and conditions, including the extent of representation in either House of the Parliament, as it thinks fit.

New States may be admitted or established.

Government of territories. **122.** The Parliament may make laws for the government of any territory surrendered by any State to and accepted by the Commonwealth, or of any territory placed by the Queen under the authority of and accepted by the Commonwealth, or otherwise acquired by the Commonwealth, and may allow the representation of such territory in either House of the Parliament to the extent and on the terms which it thinks fit.

Alteration of limits of States. **123.** The Parliament of the Commonwealth may, with the consent of the Parliament of a State, and the approval of the majority of the electors of the State voting upon the question, increase, diminish, or otherwise alter the limits of the State, upon such terms and conditions as may be agreed on, and may, with the like consent, make provision respecting the effect and operation of any increase or diminution or alteration of territory in relation to any State affected.

Formation of new States. **124.** A new State may be formed by separation of territory from a State, but only with the consent of the Parliament thereof, and a new State may be formed by the union of two or more States or parts of States, but only with the consent of the Parliaments of the States affected.

Chap. VII. Miscellaneous.

CHAPTER VII.

MISCELLANEOUS.

Seat of Government. **125.** The seat of Government of the Commonwealth shall be determined by the Parliament, and shall be within territory which shall have been granted to or acquired by the Commonwealth, and shall be vested in and belong to the Commonwealth, and shall be in the State of New South Wales, and be distant not less than one hundred miles from Sydney.

Such territory shall contain an area of not less than one hundred square miles, and such portion thereof as shall consist of Crown lands shall be granted to the Commonwealth without any payment therefor.

The Parliament shall sit at Melbourne until it meet at the seat of Government.

Power to Her Majesty to authorise Governor-General to appoint deputies. **126.** The Queen may authorise the Governor-General to appoint any person, or any persons jointly or severally, to be his deputy or deputies[14] within any part of the Commonwealth, and in that capacity to exercise during the pleasure of the Governor-General such powers and functions of the Governor-General as he thinks fit to assign to such deputy or deputies, subject to any limitations expressed or directions given by the Queen; but the appointment of such deputy or deputies shall not affect the exercise by the Governor-General himself of any power or function.

Section 127
repealed by
No. 55, 1967,
s. 3.

CHAPTER VIII.

ALTERATION OF THE CONSTITUTION.

Chap. VIII.
Alteration of
Constitution.

128.[1] This Constitution shall not be altered except in the following manner:—

Mode of
altering the
Constitution.

The proposed law for the alteration thereof must be passed by an absolute majority of each House of the Parliament, and not less than two nor more than six months after its passage through both Houses the proposed law shall be submitted in each State **and Territory** to the electors qualified to vote for the election of members of the House of Representatives.

Paragraph
altered by
No. 84, 1977,
s. 2.

But if either House passes any such proposed law by an absolute majority, and the other House rejects or fails to pass it, or passes it with any amendment to which the first-mentioned House will not agree, and if after an interval of three months the first-mentioned House in the same or the next session again passes the proposed law by an absolute majority with or without any amendment which has been made or agreed to by the other House, and such other House rejects or fails to pass it or passes it with any amendment to which the first-mentioned House will not agree, the Governor-General may submit the proposed law as last proposed by the first-mentioned House, and either with or without any amendments subsequently agreed to by both Houses, to the electors in each State **and Territory** qualified to vote for the election of the House of Representatives.

Paragraph
altered by
No. 84, 1977,
s. 2.

When a proposed law is submitted to the electors the vote shall be taken in such manner as the Parliament prescribes. But until the qualification of electors of members of the House of Representatives becomes uniform throughout the Commonwealth, only one-half the electors voting for and against the proposed law shall be counted in any State in which adult suffrage prevails.

And if in a majority of the States a majority of the electors voting approve the proposed law, and if a majority of all the electors voting also approve the proposed law, it shall be presented to the Governor-General for the Queen's assent.

No alteration diminishing the proportionate representation of any State in either House of the Parliament, or the minimum number of representatives of a State in the House of Representatives, or increasing, diminishing, or otherwise altering the limits of the State, or in any manner affecting the provisions of the Constitution in relation thereto, shall become law unless the majority of the electors voting in that State approve the proposed law.

Paragraph
added by No. 84.
1977. s. 2.

In this section, "Territory" means any territory referred to in section one hundred and twenty-two of this Constitution in respect of which there is in force a law allowing its representation in the House of Representatives.

SCHEDULE.

OATH.

I, *A.B.*, do swear that I will be faithful and bear true allegiance to Her Majesty Queen Victoria, Her heirs and successors according to law. SO HELP ME GOD!

AFFIRMATION.

I, *A.B.*, do solemnly and sincerely affirm and declare that I will be faithful and bear true allegiance to Her Majesty Queen Victoria, Her heirs and successors according to law.

(NOTE.—*The name of the King or Queen of the United Kingdom of Great Britain and Ireland for the time being is to be substituted from time to time.*)

NOTES

1. The Constitution as printed above contains all the alterations of the Constitution made up to 31 October 1986. Particulars of the Acts by which the Constitution was altered are as follows:

Act	Number and year	Date of Assent
Constitution Alteration (Senate Elections) 1906 . . .	1, 1907	3 Apr 1907
Constitution Alteration (State Debts) 1909	3, 1910	6 Aug 1910
Constitution Alteration (State Debts) 1928	1, 1929	13 Feb 1929
Constitution Alteration (Social Services) 1946 . . .	81, 1946	19 Dec 1946
Constitution Alteration (Aboriginals) 1967	55, 1967	10 Aug 1967
Constitution Alteration (Senate Casual Vacancies) 1977	82, 1977	29 July 1977
Constitution Alteration (Retirement of Judges) 1977 .	83, 1977	29 July 1977
Constitution Alteration (Referendums) 1977	84, 1977	29 July 1977

2. Covering Clause 3—The Proclamation under covering clause 3 was made on 17 September 1900 and is published in *Gazette* 1901, p. 1 and *infra* p. 41.

3. Covering Clause 5—*Cf.* the *Statute of Westminster Adoption Act 1942, infra* p. 47.

NOTES—*continued*

4. Covering Clause 7—The following Acts have repealed Acts passed by the Federal Council of Australasia:
Defence Act 1903 (No. 20, 1903), s. 6.
Pearl Fisheries Act 1952 (No. 8, 1952), s. 3. (*Pearl Fisheries Act 1952* repealed by *Continental Shelf (Living Natural Resources) Act 1968*, s. 3.)
Service and Execution of Process Act 1901 (No. 11, 1901), s. 2. (S. 2 subsequently repealed by *Service and Execution of Process Act 1963*, s. 3.)

5. S. 7—The number of senators for each State was increased to 12 by the *Representation Act 1983*, s. 3.

6. S. 9—The following State Acts have been passed in pursuance of the powers conferred by s. 9:

State	Number	Short title	How affected
New South Wales	No. 73, 1900	Federal Elections Act, 1900	Ss. 2, 3, 4, 5 and 6 and the Schedule repealed by No. 9, 1903; wholly repealed by No. 41, 1912
	No. 9, 1903	Senators' Elections Act, 1903	Amended by No. 75, 1912 and No. 112, 1984
	No. 75, 1912	Senators' Elections (Amendment) Act, 1912	*(Still in force)*
	No. 112, 1984	Senators' Elections (Amendment) Act, 1984	*(Still in force)*
Victoria	No. 1715	*Federal Elections Act 1900*	Repealed by No. 1860
	No. 1860	*Senate Elections (Times and Places) Act 1903*	Repealed by No. 2723
	No. 2399	*Senate Elections (Times and Places) Act 1912*	Repealed by No. 2723
	No. 2723	*Senate Elections (Times and Places) Act 1915*	Repealed by No. 3769
	No. 3769	*Senate Elections (Times and Places) Act 1928*	Repealed by No. 6365
	No. 6365	*Senate Elections Act 1958*	Amended by No. 10108
	No. 10108	*Senate Elections (Amendment) Act, 1984*	*(Still in force)*
Queensland . . .	64 Vic. No. 25	*The Parliament of the Commonwealth Elections Act and The Elections Acts 1885 to 1898 Amendment Act of 1900*	Operation exhausted
	3 Edw. VII. No. 6	*The Election of Senators Act of 1903*	Repealed by 9 Eliz. II. No. 20
	9 Eliz. II. No. 20	*The Senate Elections Act of 1960*	Amended by No. 79, 1984
	No. 79, 1984	*Senate Elections Act Amendment Act 1984*	*(Still in force)*
South Australia . .	No. 834	The Election of Senators Act, 1903	Amended by No. 4, 1978, No. 37, 1981 and No. 80, 1984
	No. 4, 1978	The Election of Senators Act Amendment Act, 1978	*(Still in force)*

NOTES—continued

State	Number	Short title	How affected
	No. 37, 1981	Election of Senators Act Amendment Act, 1981	*(Still in force)*
	No. 80, 1984	Election of Senators Act Amendment Act, 1984	*(Still in force)*
Western Australia	No. 11, 1903	*Election of Senators Act*, 1903	Amended by No. 27, 1912 and No. 86, 1984
	No. 27, 1912	*Election of Senators Amendment Act*, 1912	*(Still in force)*
	No. 86, 1984	*Election of Senators Amendment Act 1984*	*(Still in force)*
Tasmania	64 Vic. No. 59	The Federal Elections Act, 1900	Repealed by 26 Geo. V. No. 3
	3 Edw. VII. No. 5	The Election of Senators Act, 1903	Repealed by 26 Geo. V. No. 3
	26 Geo. V. No. 3	*Senate Elections Act* 1935	Amended by No. 63, 1984
	No. 63, 1984	*Senate Elections Amendment Act 1984*	*(Still in force)*

7. S. 14—For the provisions applicable upon the increase in the number of senators to 12 made by the *Representation Act 1983, see* s. 3 of that Act.

8. Section 15, before its substitution by the *Constitution Alteration (Senate Casual Vacancies) 1977*, provided as follows:

"15. If the place of a senator becomes vacant before the expiration of his term of service, the Houses of Parliament of the State for which he was chosen shall, sitting and voting together, choose a person to hold the place until the expiration of the term, or until the election of a successor as hereinafter provided, whichever first happens. But if the Houses of Parliament of the State are not in session at the time when the vacancy is notified, the Governor of the State, with the advice of the Executive Council thereof, may appoint a person to hold the place until the expiration of fourteen days after the beginning of the next session of the Parliament of the State, or until the election of a successor, whichever first happens.

"At the next general election of members of the House of Representatives, or at the next election of senators for the State, whichever first happens, a successor shall, if the term has not then expired, be chosen to hold the place from the date of his election until the expiration of the term.

"The name of any senator so chosen or appointed shall be certified by the Governor of the State to the Governor-General."

9. S. 15—The proposed law to alter the Constitution entitled "*Constitution Alteration (Simultaneous Elections) 1977*" was submitted to the electors in each State of the Commonwealth on 21 May 1977: it was not approved by a majority of all the electors voting in a majority of the States. *See Gazette* 1977, No. S100, p. 1.

10. S. 29—The following State Acts were passed in pursuance of the powers conferred by s. 29, but ceased to be in force upon the enactment of the *Commonwealth Electoral Act 1902*:

State	Number	Short title
New South Wales	No. 73, 1900	Federal Elections Act, 1900
Victoria	No. 1667	*Federal House of Representatives Victorian Electorates Act 1900*
Queensland	64 Vic. No. 25	*The Parliament of the Commonwealth Elections Act and The Elections Acts 1885 to 1898 Amendment Act of 1900*
Western Australia	64 Vic. No. 6	Federal House of Representatives Western Australian Electorates Act, 1900

NOTES—continued

11. S. 51—The following Imperial Acts extended the legislative powers of the Parliament:

Whaling Industry (Regulations) Act, 1934, s. 15

Geneva Convention Act, 1937, s. 2

Emergency Powers (Defence) Act, 1939, s. 5

Army and Air Force (Annual) Act, 1940, s. 3.

12. S. 51 (xxxvii.)—The following Acts have been passed by the Parliaments of the States to refer matters to the Parliament under section 51 (xxxvii.):

State	Number	Short title	How affected
New South Wales .	No. 65, 1915	Commonwealth Powers (War) Act, 1915	Expired 9 Jan 1921; *see* s. 5
	No. 33, 1942	Commonwealth Powers Act, 1942	Expired; *see* s. 4
	No. 18, 1943	Commonwealth Powers Act, 1943	Expired; *see* s. 4
	No. 48, 1983	Commonwealth Powers (Meat Inspection) Act, 1983	*(Still in force)*
Victoria	No. 3108	*Commonwealth Powers (Air Navigation) Act* 1920	Repealed by No. 4502
	No. 3658	*Commonwealth Arrangements Act* 1928 (Part III)	Repealed by No. 4502
	No. 4009	*Debt Conversion Agreement Act* 1931 (No. 2)	*(Still in force)*
	No. 4950	*Commonwealth Powers Act* 1943	Not proclaimed to come into operation and cannot now be so proclaimed
Queensland. . . .	12 Geo. V. No. 30	*The Commonwealth Powers (Air Navigation) Act* of 1921	Repealed by 1 Geo. VI. No. 8
	22 Geo. V. No. 30	*The Commonwealth Legislative Power Act*, 1931	Repealed by No. 46, 1983
	7 Geo. VI. No. 19	*Commonwealth Powers Act* 1943	Expired; *see* s. 4
	14 Geo. VI. No. 2	*The Commonwealth Powers (Air Transport) Act of* 1950	*(Still in force)*
South Australia . .	No. 1469, 1921	Commonwealth Powers (Air Navigation) Act, 1921	Repealed by No. 2352, 1937
	No. 2061, 1931	Commonwealth Legislative Power Act, 1931	*(Still in force)*
	No. 3, 1943	Commonwealth Powers Act 1943	Expired; *see* s. 5
Western Australia .	No. 4, 1943	*Commonwealth Powers Act*, 1943	Repealed by No. 58, 1965
	No. 57, 1945	*Commonwealth Powers Act*, 1945	Repealed by No. 58, 1965
	No. 30, 1947	*Commonwealth Powers Act, 1943, Amendment Act*, 1947	Repealed by No. 58, 1965

NOTES—continued

State	Number	Short title	How affected
	No. 31, 1947	*Commonwealth Powers Act, 1945, Amendment Act, 1947*	Repealed by No. 58, 1965
	No. 73, 1947	*Commonwealth Powers Act, 1945, Amendment Act, (No. 2), 1947*	Repealed by No. 58, 1965
	No. 81, 1947	*Commonwealth Powers Act, 1945-1947, Amendment (Continuance) Act, 1947*	Repealed by No. 58, 1965
Tasmania	11 Geo. V. No. 42	*Commonwealth Powers (Air Navigation) Act, 1920*	Repealed by 1 Geo. VI. No. 14
	No. 46, 1952	*Commonwealth Powers (Air Transport) Act 1952*	*(Still in force)*
	No. 62, 1966	*Commonwealth Powers (Trade Practices) Act 1966*	Expired; *see* s. 2

13. S. 74—*See Privy Council (Limitation of Appeals) Act 1968, Privy Council (Appeals from the High Court) Act 1975* and Kirmani v Captain Cook Cruises Pty Ltd (No. 2); Ex parte Attorney-General (QLD) (1985) 58 ALR 108.

14. S. 126—*See* clause IV of the Letters Patent relating to the Office of Governor-General, published in *Gazette* 1984, S334, pp. 3 and 4 and *infra* p. 44.

15. Section 127, before its repeal by the *Constitution Alteration (Aboriginals) 1967*, provided as follows:

"127. In reckoning the numbers of the people of the Commonwealth, or of a State or other part of the Commonwealth, aboriginal natives shall not be counted."

PROCLAMATION UNITING THE PEOPLE OF NEW SOUTH WALES, VICTORIA, SOUTH AUSTRALIA, QUEENSLAND, TASMANIA, AND WESTERN AUSTRALIA IN A FEDERAL COMMONWEALTH.

(*Imperial Statutory Rules and Orders, Revised* 1948, Vol. II.,
Australia, p. 1027.)

1900 No. 722.

AT THE COURT AT BALMORAL,

The 17th day of September, 1900.

PRESENT:

The Queen's Most Excellent Majesty in Council.

The following Draft Proclamation was this day read at the Board and approved:—

A. W. FITZROY.

BY THE QUEEN.

PROCLAMATION

WHEREAS by an Act of Parliament passed in the sixty-third and sixty-fourth years of Our Reign intituled, "An Act to constitute the Commonwealth of Australia," it is enacted that it shall be lawful for the Queen, with the advice of the Privy Council, to declare by proclamation that, on and after a day appointed, not being later than one year after the passing of this Act, the people of New South Wales, Victoria, South Australia, Queensland, and Tasmania, and also, if Her Majesty is satisfied that the people of Western Australia have agreed thereto, of Western Australia, shall be united in a Federal Commonwealth under the name of the Commonwealth of Australia:

And whereas We are satisfied that the people of Western Australia have agreed thereto accordingly:

We, therefore, by and with the advice of Our Privy Council, have thought fit to issue this Our Royal Proclamation, and We do hereby declare that on and after the first day of January, One thousand nine hundred and one, the people of New South Wales, Victoria, South Australia, Queensland, Tasmania, and Western Australia shall be united in a Federal Commonwealth under the name of the Commonwealth of Australia.

Given at Our Court at Balmoral, this seventeenth day of September, in the year of Our Lord One thousand nine hundred and in the sixty-fourth year of Our Reign.

GOD SAVE THE QUEEN!

Letters Patent
Relating to the Office of Governor-General of the Commonwealth of Australia

ELIZABETH THE SECOND, by the Grace of God Queen of Australia and Her other Realms and Territories, Head of the Commonwealth,

Greeting:

WHEREAS, by the Constitution of the Commonwealth of Australia, certain powers, functions and authorities are vested in a Governor-General appointed by the Queen to be Her Majesty's representative in the Commonwealth:

AND WHEREAS, by Letters Patent dated 29 October 1900, as amended, provision was made in relation to the office of Governor-General:

AND WHEREAS, by section 4 of the Constitution of the Commonwealth, the provisions of the Constitution relating to the Governor-General extend and apply to the Governor-General for the time being, or such person as the Queen may appoint to administer the Government of the Commonwealth:

AND WHEREAS We are desirous of making new provisions relating to the office of Governor-General and for persons appointed to administer the Government of the Commonwealth:

NOW THEREFORE, by these Letters Patent under Our Sign Manual and the Great Seal of Australia—

I. We revoke the Letters Patent dated 29 October 1900, as amended, and Our Instructions to the Governor-General dated 29 October 1900, as amended.

II. We declare that—

(a) the appointment of a person to the office of Governor-General shall be during Our pleasure by Commission under Our Sign Manual and the Great Seal of Australia; and

(b) before assuming office, a person appointed to be Governor-General shall take the Oath or Affirmation of Allegiance and the Oath or Affirmation of Office in the presence of the Chief Justice or another Justice of the High Court of Australia.

III. We declare that—

(a) the appointment of a person to administer the Government of the Commonwealth under section 4 of the Constitution of the Commonwealth shall be during Our pleasure by Commission under Our Sign Manual and the Great Seal of Australia;

(b) the powers, functions and authorities of the Governor-General shall, subject to this Clause, vest in any person so appointed from time to time by Us to administer the Government of the Commonwealth only in the event of the absence out of Australia, or the death, incapacity or removal, of the Governor-General for the time being;

(c) a person so appointed shall not assume the administration of the Government of the Commonwealth—

   (i) in the event of the absence of the Governor-General out of Australia—except at the request of the Governor-General or the Prime Minister of the Commonwealth;

   (ii) in the event of the absence of the Governor-General out of Australia and of the death, incapacity or absence out of Australia of the Prime Minister of the Commonwealth— except at the request of the Governor-General, the Deputy Prime Minister or the next most senior Minister of State for the Commonwealth who is in Australia and available to make such a request;

   (iii) in the event of the death, incapacity or removal of the Governor-General—except at the request of the Prime Minister of the Commonwealth; or

   (iv) in the event of the death, incapacity or removal of the Governor-General and of the death, incapacity or absence out of Australia of the Prime Minister of the Commonwealth— except at the request of the Deputy Prime Minister or the next most senior Minister of State for the Commonwealth who is in Australia and available to make such a request;

(d) a person so appointed shall not assume the administration of the Government of the Commonwealth unless he has taken on that occasion or has previously taken the Oath or Affirmation of Allegiance and the Oath or Affirmation of Office in the presence of the Chief Justice or another Justice of the High Court of Australia;

(e) a person so appointed shall cease to exercise and perform the powers, functions and authorities of the Governor-General vested in him when a successor to the Governor-General has taken the prescribed oaths or affirmations and has entered upon the duties of his office, or the incapacity or absence out of Australia of the Governor-General for the time being has ceased, as the case may be; and

(f) for the purposes of this clause, a reference to absence out of Australia is a reference to absence out of Australia in a geographical sense but does not include absence out of Australia for the purpose of visiting a Territory that is under the administration of the Commonwealth of Australia.

IV. In pursuance of section 126 of the Constitution of the Commonwealth of Australia—

(a) We authorize the Governor-General for the time being, by instrument in writing, to appoint any person, or any persons jointly or severally, to be his deputy or deputies within any part of the Commonwealth, to exercise in that capacity, during his pleasure, such powers and functions of the Governor-General as he thinks fit to assign to him or them by the instrument, but subject to the limitations expressed in this clause; and

(b) We declare that a person who is so appointed to be deputy of the Governor-General shall not exercise a power or function of the Governor-General assigned to him on any occasion—

(i) except in accordance with the instrument of appointment;

(ii) except at the request of the Governor-General or the person for the time being administering the Government of the Commonwealth that he exercise that power or function on that occasion; and

(iii) unless he has taken on that occasion or has previously taken the Oath or Affirmation of Allegiance in the presence of the Governor-General, the Chief Justice or another Justice of the High Court of Australia or the Chief Judge or another Judge of the Federal Court of Australia or of the Supreme Court of a State or Territory of the Commonwealth.

V. For the purposes of these Letters Patent—

(a) a reference to the Oath or Affirmation of Allegiance is a reference to the Oath or Affirmation in accordance with the form set out in the Schedule to the Constitution of the Commonwealth of Australia; and

(b) a reference to the Oath or Affirmation of Office is a reference to an Oath or Affirmation swearing or affirming well and truly to serve Us, Our heirs and successors according to law in the particular office and to do right to all manner of people after the laws and usages of the Commonwealth of Australia, without fear or favour, affection or illwill.

VI. We direct that these Letters Patent, each Commission appointing a Governor-General or person to administer the Government of the Commonwealth of Australia and each instrument of appointment of a deputy of the Governor-General shall be published in the official gazette of the Commonwealth of Australia.

VII. We further direct that these Letters Patent shall take effect without affecting the efficacy of any Commission or appointment given or made before the date hereof or of anything done in pursuance of any such Commission or appointment, or of any oath or affirmation taken before that date for the purpose of any such Commission or appointment.

VIII. We reserve full power from time to time to revoke, alter or amend these Letters Patent as We think fit.

GIVEN at Our Court

at Balmoral

on 21 August 1984

By Her Majesty's Command,

BOB HAWKE

Prime Minister

STATUTE OF WESTMINSTER
ADOPTION ACT 1942

An Act to remove Doubts as to the Validity of certain Commonwealth Legislation, to obviate Delays occurring in its Passage, and to effect certain related purposes, by adopting certain Sections of the Statute of Westminster, 1931, as from the Commencement of the War between His Majesty the King and Germany.

Preamble

WHEREAS certain legal difficulties exist which have created doubts and caused delays in relation to certain Commonwealth legislation, and to certain regulations made thereunder, particularly in relation to the legislation enacted, and regulations made, for securing the public safety and defence of the Commonwealth of Australia, and for the more effectual prosecution of the war in which His Majesty the King is engaged:

AND WHEREAS those legal difficulties will be removed by the adoption by the Parliament of the Commonwealth of Australia of sections two, three, four, five and six of the Statute of Westminster, 1931, and by making such adoption have effect as from the commencement of the war between His Majesty the King and Germany:

BE it therefore enacted by the King's Most Excellent Majesty, the Senate, and the House of Representatives of the Commonwealth of Australia, as follows:

Short title

1. This Act may be cited as the *Statute of Westminster Adoption Act 1942.*[1]

Commencement

2. This Act shall come into operation on the day on which it receives the Royal Assent.[1]

Adoption of Statute of Westminster, 1931

3. Sections two, three, four, five and six of the Imperial Act entitled the Statute of Westminster, 1931 (which Act is set out in the Schedule to this Act) are adopted and the adoption shall have effect from the third day of September, One thousand nine hundred and thirty-nine.

THE SCHEDULE   Section 3

STATUTE OF WESTMINSTER, 1931.

An Act to give effect to certain resolutions passed by Imperial Conferences held in the years 1926 and 1930.

[11th December, 1931.]

WHEREAS the delegates of His Majesty's Governments in the United Kingdom, the Dominion of Canada, the Commonwealth of Australia, the Dominion of New Zealand, the Union of South Africa, the Irish Free State and Newfoundland, at Imperial Conferences holden at Westminster in the years of our Lord nineteen hundred and twenty-six and nineteen hundred and thirty did concur in making the declarations and resolutions set forth in the Reports of the said Conferences:

AND WHEREAS it is meet and proper to set out by way of preamble to this Act that, inasmuch as the Crown is the symbol of the free association of the members of the British Commonwealth of Nations, and as they are united by a common allegiance to the Crown, it would be in accord with the established constitutional position of all the members of the Commonwealth in relation to one another that any alteration in the law touching the Succession to the Throne or the Royal Style and Titles shall hereafter require the assent as well of the Parliaments of all the Dominions as of the Parliament of the United Kingdom:

AND WHEREAS it is in accord with the established constitutional position that no law hereafter made by the Parliament of the United Kingdom shall extend to any of the said Dominions as part of the law of that Dominion otherwise than at the request and with the consent of that Dominion:

AND WHEREAS it is necessary for the ratifying, confirming and establishing of certain of the said declarations and resolutions of the said Conferences that a law be made and enacted in due form by authority of the Parliament of the United Kingdom:

AND WHEREAS the Dominion of Canada, the Commonwealth of Australia, the Dominion of New Zealand, the Union of South Africa, the Irish Free State and Newfoundland have severally requested and consented to the submission of a measure to the Parliament of the United Kingdom for making such provision with regard to the matters aforesaid as is hereafter in this Act contained:

NOW, THEREFORE, be it enacted by the King's Most Excellent Majesty by and with the advice and consent of the Lords Spiritual and Temporal, and Commons, in this present Parliament assembled, and by the authority of the same, as follows:—

Meaning of "Dominion" in this Act.

1. In this Act the expression "Dominion" means any of the following Dominions, that is to say, the Dominion of Canada, the Commonwealth of Australia, the Dominion of New Zealand, the Union of South Africa, the Irish Free State and Newfoundland.

Validity of laws made by Parliament of a Dominion.
28 and 29 Vict. c. 63.

2.—(1) The Colonial Laws Validity Act, 1865, shall not apply to any law made after the commencement of this Act by the Parliament of a Dominion.

(2) No law and no provision of any law made after the commencement of this Act by the Parliament of a Dominion shall be void or inoperative on the ground that it is repugnant to the law of England, or to the provisions of any existing or future Act of Parliament of the United Kingdom, or to any order, rule or regulation made under any such Act, and the powers of the Parliament of a Dominion shall include the power to repeal or amend any such Act, order, rule or regulation in so far as the same is part of the law of the Dominion.

Power of Parliament of Dominion to legislate extra-territorially.

3. It is hereby declared and enacted that the Parliament of a Dominion has full power to make laws having extra-territorial operation.

Parliament of United Kingdom not to legislate for Dominion except by consent.

4. *No Act of Parliament of the United Kingdom passed after the commencement of this Act shall extend, or be deemed to extend, to a Dominion as part of the law of that Dominion, unless it is expressly declared in that Act that that Dominion has requested, and consented to, the enactment thereof.*[2]

Powers of Dominion Parliaments in relation to merchant shipping.
57 and 58 Vict. c. 60.

5. Without prejudice to the generality of the foregoing provisions of this Act, sections seven hundred and thirty-five and seven hundred and thirty-six of the Merchant Shipping Act, 1894, shall be construed as though reference therein to the Legislature of a British possession did not include reference to the Parliament of a Dominion.

6. Without prejudice to the generality of the foregoing provisions of this Act, section four of the Colonial Courts of Admiralty Act, 1890 (which requires certain laws to be reserved for the signification of His Majesty's pleasure or to contain a suspending clause), and so much of section seven of that Act as requires the approval of His Majesty in Council to any rules of Court for regulating the practice and procedure of a Colonial Court of Admiralty, shall cease to have effect in any Dominion as from the commencement of this Act.

Powers of Dominion Parliaments in relation to Courts of Admiralty.
53 and 54 Vict. c. 27.

7.—(1) Nothing in this Act shall be deemed to apply to the repeal, amendment or alteration of the British North America Acts, 1867 to 1930, or any order, rule or regulation made thereunder.

Saving for British North America Acts and application of the Act to Canada.

(2) The provisions of section two of this Act shall extend to laws made by any of the Provinces of Canada and to the powers of the legislatures of such Provinces.

(3) The powers conferred by this Act upon the Parliament of Canada or upon the legislatures of the Provinces shall be restricted to the enactment of laws in relation to matters within the competence of the Parliament of Canada, or of any of the legislatures of the Provinces respectively.

8. Nothing in this Act shall be deemed to confer any power to repeal or alter the Constitution or the Constitution Act of the Commonwealth of Australia or the Constitution Act of the Dominion of New Zealand otherwise than in accordance with the law existing before the commencement of this Act.

Saving for Constitution Acts of Australia and New Zealand.

9.—(1) Nothing in this Act shall be deemed to authorize the Parliament of the Commonwealth of Australia to make laws on any matter within the authority of the States of Australia, not being a matter within the authority of the Parliament or Government of the Commonwealth of Australia.

Saving with respect to States of Australia.

(2) *Nothing in this Act shall be deemed to require the concurrence of the Parliament or Government of the Commonwealth of Australia in any law made by the Parliament of the United Kingdom with respect to any matter within the authority of the States of Australia, not being a matter within the authority of the Parliament or Government of the Commonwealth of Australia, in any case where it would have been in accordance with the constitutional practice existing before the commencement of this Act that the Parliament of the United Kingdom should make that law without such concurrence.[2]*

(3) *In the application of this Act to the Commonwealth of Australia the request and consent referred to in section four shall mean the request and consent of the Parliament and Government of the Commonwealth.[2]*

10.—(1) None of the following sections of this Act, that is to say, sections two, three, four, five and six, shall extend to a Dominion to which this section applies as part of the law of that Dominion unless that section is adopted by the Parliament of the Dominion, and any Act of that Parliament adopting any section of this Act may provide that the adoption shall have effect either from the commencement of this Act or from such later date as is specified in the adopting Act.

Certain sections of Act not to apply to Australia, New Zealand or Newfoundland unless adopted.

(2) *The Parliament of any such Dominion as aforesaid may at any time revoke the adoption of any section referred to in sub-section (1) of this section.[2]*

(3) The Dominions to which this section applies are the Commonwealth of Australia, the Dominion of New Zealand and Newfoundland.

11. Notwithstanding anything in the Interpretation Act, 1889, the expression "Colony" shall not, in any Act of the Parliament of the United Kingdom passed after the commencement of this Act, include a Dominion or any Province or State forming part of a Dominion.

Meaning of "Colony" in future Acts.
52 and 53 Vict. c. 63.

12. This Act may be cited as the Statute of Westminster, 1931.

Short title.

NOTES

1. Act No. 56, 1942; assented to 9 October 1942.

2. Sections 4, 9 (2) and (3) and 10 (2) of the Statute of Westminster 1931, in so far as they were part of the law of the Commonwealth, of a State or of a Territory, have been repealed by section 12 of the *Australia Act 1986*.
The Parliament of the Commonwealth of Australia has on three occasions passed Acts requesting and consenting to the enactment by the Parliament of

NOTES—*continued*

the United Kingdom of Acts extending to Australia. The Acts of the Parliaments of the Commonwealth and of the United Kingdom, respectively, are as follows:

Australia	United Kingdom
Australia (Request and Consent) Act 1985	Australia Act 1986
Christmas Island (Request and Consent) Act 1957 . .	Christmas Island Act, 1958
Cocos (Keeling) Islands (Request and Consent) Act 1954	Cocos Islands Act, 1955

AUSTRALIA ACT 1986

TABLE OF PROVISIONS

AUSTRALIA ACT 1986

An Act to bring constitutional arrangements affecting the Commonwealth and the States into conformity with the status of the Commonwealth of Australia as a sovereign, independent and federal nation

WHEREAS the Prime Minister of the Commonwealth and the Premiers of the States at conferences held in Canberra on 24 and 25 June 1982 and 21 June 1984 agreed on the taking of certain measures to bring constitutional arrangements affecting the Commonwealth and the States into conformity with the status of the Commonwealth of Australia as a sovereign, independent and federal nation:

AND WHEREAS in pursuance of paragraph 51 (xxxviii) of the Constitution the Parliaments of all the States have requested the Parliament of the Commonwealth to enact an Act in the terms of this Act:

BE IT THEREFORE ENACTED by the Queen, and the Senate and the House of Representatives of the Commonwealth of Australia, as follows:

Termination of power of Parliament of United Kingdom to legislate for Australia

1. No Act of the Parliament of the United Kingdom passed after the commencement of this Act shall extend, or be deemed to extend, to the Commonwealth, to a State or to a Territory as part of the law of the Commonwealth, of the State or of the Territory.

Legislative powers of Parliaments of States

2. (1) It is hereby declared and enacted that the legislative powers of the Parliament of each State include full power to make laws for the peace, order and good government of that State that have extra-territorial operation.

(2) It is hereby further declared and enacted that the legislative powers of the Parliament of each State include all legislative powers that the Parliament of the United Kingdom might have exercised before the commencement of this Act for the peace, order and good government of that State but nothing in this subsection confers on a State any capacity that the State did not have immediately before the commencement of this Act to engage in relations with countries outside Australia.

Termination of restrictions on legislative powers of Parliaments of States

3. (1) The Act of the Parliament of the United Kingdom known as the Colonial Laws Validity Act 1865 shall not apply to any law made after the commencement of this Act by the Parliament of a State.

(2) No law and no provision of any law made after the commencement of this Act by the Parliament of a State shall be void or inoperative on the ground that it is repugnant to the law of England, or to the provisions of any existing or future Act of the Parliament of the United Kingdom, or to any order, rule or regulation made under any such Act, and the powers of the Parliament of a State shall include the power to repeal or amend any such Act, order, rule or regulation in so far as it is part of the law of the State.

Powers of State Parliaments in relation to merchant shipping

4. Sections 735 and 736 of the Act of the Parliament of the United Kingdom known as the Merchant Shipping Act 1894, in so far as they are part of the law of a State, are hereby repealed.

Commonwealth Constitution, Constitution Act and Statute of Westminster not affected

5. Sections 2 and 3 (2) above—

(a) are subject to the Commonwealth of Australia Constitution Act and to the Constitution of the Commonwealth; and

(b) do not operate so as to give any force or effect to a provision of an Act of the Parliament of a State that would repeal, amend or be repugnant to this Act, the Commonwealth of Australia Constitution Act, the Constitution of the Commonwealth or the Statute of Westminster 1931 as amended and in force from time to time.

Manner and form of making certain State laws

6. Notwithstanding sections 2 and 3 (2) above, a law made after the commencement of this Act by the Parliament of a State respecting the constitution, powers or procedure of the Parliament of the State shall be of no force or effect unless it is made in such manner and form as may from time to time be required by a law made by that Parliament, whether made before or after the commencement of this Act.

Powers and functions of Her Majesty and Governors in respect of States

7. (1) Her Majesty's representative in each State shall be the Governor.

(2) Subject to subsections (3) and (4) below, all powers and functions of Her Majesty in respect of a State are exercisable only by the Governor of the State.

(3) Subsection (2) above does not apply in relation to the power to appoint, and the power to terminate the appointment of, the Governor of a State.

(4) While Her Majesty is personally present in a State, Her Majesty is not precluded from exercising any of Her powers and functions in respect of the State that are the subject of subsection (2) above.

(5) The advice to Her Majesty in relation to the exercise of the powers and functions of Her Majesty in respect of a State shall be tendered by the Premier of the State.

State laws not subject to disallowance or suspension of operation

8. An Act of the Parliament of a State that has been assented to by the Governor of the State shall not, after the commencement of this Act, be subject to disallowance by Her Majesty, nor shall its operation be suspended pending the signification of Her Majesty's pleasure thereon.

State laws not subject to withholding of assent or reservation

9. (1) No law or instrument shall be of any force or effect in so far as it purports to require the Governor of a State to withhold assent from any Bill for an Act of the State that has been passed in such manner and form as may from time to time be required by a law made by the Parliament of the State.

(2) No law or instrument shall be of any force or effect in so far as it purports to require the reservation of any Bill for an Act of a State for the signification of Her Majesty's pleasure thereon.

Termination of responsibility of United Kingdom Government in relation to State matters

10. After the commencement of this Act Her Majesty's Government in the United Kingdom shall have no responsibility for the government of any State.

Termination of appeals to Her Majesty in Council

11. (1) Subject to subsection (4) below, no appeal to Her Majesty in Council lies or shall be brought, whether by leave or special leave of any court or of Her Majesty in Council or otherwise, and whether by virtue of any Act of the Parliament of the United Kingdom, the Royal Prerogative or otherwise, from or in respect of any decision of an Australian court.

(2) Subject to subsection (4) below—

(a) the enactments specified in subsection (3) below and any orders, rules, regulations or other instruments made under, or for the purposes of, those enactments; and

(b) any other provisions of Acts of the Parliament of the United Kingdom in force immediately before the commencement of this Act that make provision for or in relation to appeals to

Her Majesty in Council from or in respect of decisions of courts, and any orders, rules, regulations or other instruments made under, or for the purposes of, any such provisions,

in so far as they are part of the law of the Commonwealth, of a State or of a Territory, are hereby repealed.

(3) The enactments referred to in subsection (2) (a) above are the following Acts of the Parliament of the United Kingdom or provisions of such Acts:

The Australian Courts Act 1828, section 15

The Judicial Committee Act 1833

The Judicial Committee Act 1844

The Australian Constitutions Act 1850, section 28

The Colonial Courts of Admiralty Act 1890, section 6.

(4) Nothing in the foregoing provisions of this section—

(a) affects an appeal instituted before the commencement of this Act to Her Majesty in Council from or in respect of a decision of an Australian court; or

(b) precludes the institution after that commencement of an appeal to Her Majesty in Council from or in respect of such a decision where the appeal is instituted—

(i) pursuant to leave granted by an Australian court on an application made before that commencement; or

(ii) pursuant to special leave granted by Her Majesty in Council on a petition presented before that commencement,

but this subsection shall not be construed as permitting or enabling an appeal to Her Majesty in Council to be instituted or continued that could not have been instituted or continued if this section had not been enacted.

Amendment of Statute of Westminster

12. Sections 4, 9 (2) and (3) and 10 (2) of the Statute of Westminster 1931, in so far as they are part of the law of the Commonwealth, of a State or of a Territory, are hereby repealed.

Amendment of Constitution Act of Queensland

13. (1) The Constitution Act 1867-1978 of the State of Queensland is in this section referred to as the Principal Act.

(2) Section 11A of the Principal Act is amended in subsection (3)—

(a) by omitting from paragraph (a)—

(i) "and Signet"; and

      (ii) "constituted under Letters Patent under the Great Seal of the United Kingdom"; and

(b) by omitting from paragraph (b)—

      (i) "and Signet"; and

      (ii) "whenever and so long as the office of Governor is vacant or the Governor is incapable of discharging the duties of administration or has departed from Queensland".

(3) Section 11B of the Principal Act is amended—

(a) by omitting "Governor to conform to instructions" and substituting "Definition of Royal Sign Manual";

(b) by omitting subsection (1); and

(c) by omitting from subsection (2)—

      (i) "(2)";

      (ii) "this section and in"; and

      (iii) "and the expression 'Signet' means the seal commonly used for the sign manual of the Sovereign or the seal with which documents are sealed by the Secretary of State in the United Kingdom on behalf of the Sovereign".

(4) Section 14 of the Principal Act is amended in subsection (2) by omitting ", subject to his performing his duty prescribed by section 11B,".

Amendment of Constitution Act of Western Australia

    14. (1) The Constitution Act 1889 of the State of Western Australia is in this section referred to as the Principal Act.

(2) Section 50 of the Principal Act is amended in subsection (3)—

(a) by omitting from paragraph (a)—

      (i) "and Signet"; and

      (ii) "constituted under Letters Patent under the Great Seal of the United Kingdom";

(b) by omitting from paragraph (b)—

      (i) "and signet"; and

      (ii) "whenever and so long as the office of Governor is vacant or the Governor is incapable of discharging the duties of administration or has departed from Western Australia"; and

(c) by omitting from paragraph (c)—

      (i) "under the Great Seal of the United Kingdom"; and

      (ii) "during a temporary absence of the Governor for a short period from the seat of Government or from the State".

(3) Section 51 of the Principal Act is amended—

(a) by omitting subsection (1); and

(b) by omitting from subsection (2)—

    (i) "(2)";

    (ii) "this section and in"; and

    (iii) "and the expression 'Signet' means the seal commonly used for the sign manual of the Sovereign or the seal with which documents are sealed by the Secretary of State in the United Kingdom on behalf of the Sovereign".

Method of repeal or amendment of this Act or Statute of Westminster

15. (1) This Act or the Statute of Westminster 1931, as amended and in force from time to time, in so far as it is part of the law of the Commonwealth, of a State or of a Territory, may be repealed or amended by an Act of the Parliament of the Commonwealth passed at the request or with the concurrence of the Parliaments of all the States and, subject to subsection (3) below, only in that manner.

(2) For the purposes of subsection (1) above, an Act of the Parliament of the Commonwealth that is repugnant to this Act or the Statute of Westminster 1931, as amended and in force from time to time, or to any provision of this Act or of that Statute as so amended and in force, shall, to the extent of the repugnancy, be deemed an Act to repeal or amend the Act, Statute or provision to which it is repugnant.

(3) Nothing in subsection (1) above limits or prevents the exercise by the Parliament of the Commonwealth of any powers that may be conferred upon that Parliament by any alteration to the Constitution of the Commonwealth made in accordance with section 128 of the Constitution of the Commonwealth after the commencement of this Act.

Interpretation

16. (1) In this Act, unless the contrary intention appears—

"appeal" includes a petition of appeal, and a complaint in the nature of an appeal;

"appeal to Her Majesty in Council" includes any appeal to Her Majesty;

"Australian court" means a court of a State or any other court of Australia or of a Territory other than the High Court;

"court" includes a judge, judicial officer or other person acting judicially;

"decision" includes determination, judgment, decree, order or sentence;

"Governor", in relation to a State, includes any person for the time being administering the government of the State;

"State" means a State of the Commonwealth and includes a new State;

"the Commonwealth of Australia Constitution Act" means the Act of the Parliament of the United Kingdom known as the Commonwealth of Australia Constitution Act;

"the Constitution of the Commonwealth" means the Constitution of the Commonwealth set forth in section 9 of the Commonwealth of Australia Constitution Act, being that Constitution as altered and in force from time to time;

"the Statute of Westminster 1931" means the Act of the Parliament of the United Kingdom known as the Statute of Westminster 1931.

(2) The expression "a law made by that Parliament" in section 6 above and the expression "a law made by the Parliament" in section 9 above include, in relation to the State of Western Australia, the Constitution Act 1889 of that State.

(3) A reference in this Act to the Parliament of a State includes, in relation to the State of New South Wales, a reference to the legislature of that State as constituted from time to time in accordance with the Constitution Act, 1902, or any other Act of that State, whether or not, in relation to any particular legislative act, the consent of the Legislative Council of that State is necessary.

Short title and commencement

17. (1) This Act may be cited as the *Australia Act 1986*.[1]

(2) This Act shall come into operation on a day and at a time to be fixed by Proclamation.[1]

NOTE

1. Act No. 142, 1985; assented to 4 December 1985 and came into operation on 3 March 1986 at 5.00 a.m. Greenwich Mean Time (*see Gazette* 1986, No. S85, p. 1).

In addition to this *Australia Act 1986* an Australia Act 1986, in substantially identical terms, was enacted by the United Kingdom Parliament (1986 Chapter 2) pursuant to a request made and consent given by the Parliament and Government of the Commonwealth in the *Australia (Request and Consent) Act 1986* and with the concurrence of all the States of Australia (*see* the Australia Acts Request Act 1985 of each State).

INDEX TO THE
COMMONWEALTH OF AUSTRALIA
CONSTITUTION ACT

NOTE.—In the reference to sections, the numbers to which the letters " cl. " are prefixed refer to the " covering clauses " of the Constitution Act; the numbers without that prefix refer to the sections of the Constitution.

Subject	Section	Page
COMMONWEALTH—*continued*		
legislative power of. See LEGISLATIVE POWER OF COMMONWEALTH.		
Ministers of State for. See MINISTERS OF STATE FOR THE COMMONWEALTH.		
name of	cl. 3	5
not to abridge reasonable use of rivers	100	30
give preference to State or part	99	30
legislate as to religion	116	33
tax State property	114	33
officers of. See OFFICERS.		
Parliament of. See PARLIAMENT OF THE COMMONWEALTH.		
parts of. See PARTS OF THE COMMONWEALTH.		
party to suit, jurisdiction where	75 (iii.)	25
people of. See PEOPLE.		
person suing or sued on behalf of, jurisdiction where	75 (iii.)	25
See also FEDERAL JURISDICTION.		
proceedings against, rights may be conferred	78	25
property of, not taxable by States without consent	114	33
protection of States by	119	33
revenue of. See REVENUE.		
seat of Government of. See SEAT OF GOVERNMENT.		
States are part of	cl. 6	6
statistics of. See STATISTICS.		
COMPENSATION		
for property acquired under Commonwealth laws	51 (xxxi.)	18
territory of seat of Government	125	34
to officers of transferred departments not retained	84	26
State, for property of transferred departments	85 (iii.)	27
CONCILIATION, INDUSTRIAL—		
legislative power as to	51 (xxxv.)	18
CONCURRENT		
legislative power, of States	107	32
State laws within, continuance of	108	32
See also LEGISLATIVE POWER OF STATES.		
CONSERVATION		
of water, right to reasonable use of rivers for, not to be abridged	100	30
CONSOLIDATED REVENUE FUND—		
all revenues or moneys raised or received, to form	81	26
appropriation of	81, 83	26
charges upon and application of	82	26
salary of Governor-General payable from	3	7
Ministers payable from	66	22
See also REVENUE.		
CONSTITUTION		
Act, binding effect of	cl. 5	6
of Commonwealth, agreements with respect to public debts of States binding on parties notwithstanding	105A (5.)	31
alterations of	128	35
commencement of	cl. 4	5
Commonwealth is under	Preamble	5
division of	cl. 9	6
execution and maintenance of	61	21
laws made under, binding effect of	cl. 5	6
matters arising under or involving interpretation of, jurisdiction in	76 (i.), 77	25
See also FEDERAL JURISDICTION.		
of State. See STATES, THE.		
CONSTITUTIONAL POWERS		
of Commonwealth and States, appeal from High Court as to limits of	74	24
CONSULS—		
jurisdiction in matters affecting	75 (ii.)	25
See also FEDERAL JURISDICTION.		

* See also 51 (xxxvi.).

* See also 51 (xxxvi.).

* See also 51 (xxxvi.).

Index to Constitution